# how to register a copyright and protect your creative work

# how to registe

# protect your

A BASIC GUIDE TO THE NEW
COPYRIGHT LAW AND HOW IT
AFFECTS ANYONE WHO WANTS
TO PROTECT CREATIVE WORK

# a copyright and creative work

## Robert B. Chickering
## and Susan Hartman

**Charles Scribner's Sons** ● **New York**

Copyright © 1980  Robert B. Chickering and Susan Hartman

Library of Congress Cataloging in Publication Data

Chickering, Robert B.
How to register a copyright and protect your creative work.

Includes index.
1.   Copyright—United States.   I.   Hartman, Susan, joint
author.   II.   Title.
KF2995.C45      346.7304'82      80-23203
ISBN 0-684-16705-0

3 5 7 9 11 13 15 17 19 Y/C 20 18 16 14 12 10 8 6 4 2

Printed in the United States of America

# contents

# Introduction

Most people realize that writers, painters, sculptors, and composers are directly affected by the copyright law. However, copyright law reaches well beyond classic creative art forms. Architects, scientists, engineers, educators, lawyers, students, entertainers, business owners, advertising agents, graphic artists, and a myriad of others regularly create works that are protected by copyright.

The United States copyright law was recently revised, the first complete revision since 1909. The new law is known as the Copyright Act of 1976, but most of the provisions did not become effective until January 1, 1978. There are dramatic changes in the new copyright law substantially increasing the rights of the creators of copyrightable works.

It is an important goal of this book to inform the reader about the new copyright law, and also to enable those who want to do so to take certain steps on their own behalf to protect and perfect their rights in their creative works. Accordingly, the first half of this book is designed to guide the reader through the copyright-registration process and use of the proper notice on published copyrighted works. The second half of the book is directed to general information, frequently asked questions, and certain areas of special interest. The overall purpose is to provide sufficient background to make you aware of your rights and responsibilities as a copyright owner. Such knowledge is essential if you are to maintain control over your work, be effective in negotiations, and gain full advantage from the product of your creation. It also is crucial to know what can cause the loss of a copyright and what steps should be taken to preserve a copyright.

Although copyright registration can be performed by a nonlawyer, this book is not intended as a guide for laymen to represent themselves in legal actions. A copyright attorney always should be consulted in connection with areas other than registration and notice, and in connection with registration and notice if the procedures or requirements are not clear.

ROBERT B. CHICKERING
SUSAN HARTMAN

# 1
## before you register a claim to copyright

## IS YOUR WORK COPYRIGHTABLE?

You've written a novel or a play and you want to find out whether your work can be copyrighted and how to go about it. Or you've taken a photograph that is something special and you want to know if it can be protected under the copyright law or some other law—or not at all. The Constitution of the United States empowers Congress to grant exclusive rights to "authors" for their "writings." Copyright protection under the United States copyright law, however, has been extended by Congress to well beyond the literal meaning of the word "writings" and includes literary, musical, dramatic, artistic, and other intellectual creations or "works of authorship." Similarly, the term "authors" applies to creators of all of these forms of "writings."

A copyright is a series of exclusive, personal-property rights granted for a limited period of time to the author of an original work. Federal copyright protection exists only when the work has been fixed in a tangible medium. The exclusive rights granted to the author of an original work include the right to prohibit others from reproducing (copying), adapting (making derivative works), distributing, performing, and displaying the work.

## Types of Work That Can Be Copyrighted

The following categories are copyrightable. The list is not complete, but shows the types of "writings" subject to copyright protection. If you do not find your particular type of creation here, it is not necessarily excluded from the law, but you should be able to recognize whether your work is of the same general nature as the works in these categories:

1.  LITERARY WORKS, such as:
    (A) *Books, pamphlets, leaflets, single pages*—novels, poems, non-fiction writings, essays, catalogs, directories, compilations, anthologies, computer programs, data bases
    (B) *Periodicals*—magazines, newspapers, newsletters, bulletins, serial publications, reviews
    (C) *Contributions to periodicals*—articles, columns, cartoons, drawings, advertisements
    (D) *Scripts for oral deliveries*—lectures, addresses, speeches, sermons, panel discussions, recording scripts, monologues
2.  MUSICAL WORKS—lyrics, music, arrangements
3.  DRAMATIC WORKS—stage plays, operas, musicals, radio and television dramas
4.  PANTOMIMES AND CHOREOGRAPHIC WORKS (excluding social dance steps)
5.  PICTORIAL, GRAPHIC, AND SCULPTURAL WORKS
    (A) *Fine, graphic, and applied art*—paintings, drawings, photographs, prints, filmstrips, cartoons, slide films, art reproductions, sculpture, dolls, jewelry, enamels, glassware, wallpaper and fabric designs, tapestries, postcards, greeting cards, advertising artwork, labels
    (B) *Scientific and technical works*—engineering diagrams, mechanical and architectural drawings, models, astronomical charts, maps, marine charts, globes, anatomical models
6.  MOTION PICTURES AND AUDIOVISUAL WORKS—slide series or other series of images with accompanying sounds
7.  SOUND RECORDINGS—music, spoken sounds, sound effects

## Types of Work That Cannot Be Copyrighted

Although they may seem to be "writings" in the broadest sense of the word, some categories of works simply do not qualify for copyright protection. Again, without being totally inclusive, the following categories are representative of areas in which copyright protection is not available.

1. RECORD BOOKS, BLANK FORMS, FILL-IN ITEMS, AND OTHER WORKS THAT DO NOT COMMUNI-CATE—Many forms are relatively blank or open, and any communication or subject matter that could constitute a "writing" resides in the information that is to be filled into the form, not in the form itself. Thus, forms that are merely grids of lines or simple formats for filling in information are not copyrightable. Blank checks, for example, do not qualify for copyright protection; however, checks embellished with a pictorial design do qualify since a work of the visual arts is expressed on them. The copyright would cover the work of art, but it would not extend to the form of the blank check. Some forms contain sufficient communicative information to make them copyrightable. Thus, the mere fact that the work is a "form," or is used to collect data, or must be filled in, will not prevent copyright protection, if the work also contains a communicative "writing."

2. INFORMATION THAT IS COMMON PROPERTY—Such things as rulers, tape measures, height-and-weight charts, and calendars are not themselves copyrightable. However, if they are adapted in a way that gives them an original form of expression—for example, a calendar rendered in a decorative manner—the creative aspect added to the calendar may be copyrighted.

3. IDEAS, METHODS, SYSTEMS, AND PLANS—Although you can copyright the work of authorship in which the idea is revealed, it is the form of expression, not the idea, that is protected.

4. TITLES OF WORKS, NAMES, PEN NAMES, NAMES OF PRODUCTS AND SERVICES, NAMES OF ORGA-NIZATIONS, MOTTOS, SLOGANS, AND SHORT

PHRASES—Even though you must list a title for your work when you register it in the Copyright Office, this title is for identification purposes only, and its listing in the copyright registration does not mean that the title is copyrighted. Sometimes protection for a name or phrase can be obtained under trademark, service mark, or trade-name laws, but these areas of the law are founded upon an entirely different basis than the copyright law.

5. LIST OF INGREDIENTS—The list of ingredients on a food container is not copyrightable; however, where creativity has been added, such as in a recipe, the work may be copyrighted.

If you are unsure as to whether your work is copyrightable, assume that it is. Accordingly, when you are in doubt, you should take the steps necessary to protect your work as though it were copyrightable; namely, you should attempt to register the work, and when it is published, you should use the proper copyright notice. In borderline situations, when your application for copyright registration initially is rejected by the Copyright Office, do not merely acquiesce. Write a letter of explanation to the Copyright Office pointing out the creative expression contained in your work and how it communicates. An example of a work that was at first denied registration by the Copyright Office is a book that had pages consisting entirely of a series of numbers arranged in particular patterns. When it was explained that these patterns of numbers were designed as a teaching tool that communicated mathematical principles to pupils, the claim to copyright was registered by the Copyright Office.

# COPYRIGHT REQUIREMENTS

## Form of Expression

You may have the best idea in the world—the theme for a great book or musical score—but until you set it down in a tangible form, your idea is not protectable under the Copyright Act. In order to be protected under the Copyright Act, the idea must be fixed in a tangible medium of expression that can be perceived, reproduced, or otherwise communicated. For example, a written work, picture, or musical composition may be copyrighted, but the concept or idea for such a work cannot be copyrighted.

When you convert your idea into a fixed form, it is your form of expression—not your concept—that is protected. If it seems unfair that someone can use your ideas, a simple explanation of the reasoning behind the law is that copyright is designed to stimulate, not limit, the development of original works. The protection given by copyright is intended to encourage creativity by granting exclusive rights to the copyright owner. However, if ideas per se were copyrightable, this would restrict creative efforts. Many new forms of work often develop from a single idea into a wide range of significant works in literature, music, and fine arts. If the broad idea became the property of one person, the deprivation of society would be enormous. You may find that an idea from an external source may plant the seed for your own creation, which has an entirely different viewpoint, interpretation, and method of presentation.

There is one exception to the requirement that the work must be fixed in a tangible medium in order to have copyright protection, and that pertains to choreography, pantomime, lectures, and musical works, which are all capable of repeated performance without being reduced to a tangible form. Until they are fixed in a tangible form, these works are not protected under the Copyright Act of 1976. Nevertheless, they are protected under common-law principles of copyright law that have developed over many years of court decisions. When and if such works are expressed in a tangible form, they will then be subject to protection under the Copyright Act. Pantomime and choreography, for example, are notable new additions to the scope of copyright protection under the new law, but only when they are fixed in a tangible medium, such as film or dance notations.

## Degree of Originality

Since copyright law is designed to promote creativity and encourage the development of the arts, one of the primary requirements for copyright protection is originality of expression. This does not mean that only works of extraordinary innovation and genius are considered worthy of copyright protection. If your work is of your own creation and does not copy another's work, you need not worry that it will be disapproved by the Copyright Office because it fails to meet a test of excellence or a high degree of originality based upon some standard of artistic performance. The Copyright Office does not function as a critic and does not grant copyright registration on the basis of artistic merit. The Copyright Office does not even compare the work itself with existing works, as the Patent and Trademark Office does during its patent-searching-and-examination procedure.

When you file a copyright application, you are seeking to register a *claim* to copyright—a claim that your work is original or at least contains an element of originality. Your purpose is to create a basis for enforcement of rights in your work should others infringe upon them by using your work without your consent. It is not the purpose of the copyright registration to determine the degree of originality present in your work or to investigate whether or not you are infringing upon the rights of others.

If you have copied an earlier work that you were not legally entitled to use, and if your copy comes to the attention of the copyright owner of the earlier work, it might become the subject of a lawsuit. You could suffer the penalties for infringement and also could lose your investment in the production and distribution of copies of the work. The Copyright Office, however, does not bring such infringements to the attention of copyright owners. The copyright owner of the earlier work must discover the infringement and bring legal action.

Unless you knowingly use someone else's copyrighted work without permission, there is usually little reason to worry about infringing upon another's property rights. Normally, you cannot infringe a copyright without copying, although there is sometimes the danger that you inadvertently "copied" by recalling the work of another that was stored in your memory. Even in the very unlikely event that a work developed from your own imagination parallels an existing work so exactly in its form of expression that it would otherwise appear to infringe upon another person's copyright, theoretically, it will not be an infringement. But if you had access to the earlier work and the likeness is great, a court may not believe that your similar creation was coincidental and not copied.

# SHOULD YOU REGISTER YOUR WORK?

Your work is automatically protected by the copyright law from the moment it is created—fixed in a tangible medium—even though you have not registered it with the Copyright Office. You do not have to register a claim to copyright in your work in order to reproduce, distribute, market, transfer ownership, or license your work. So why bother to go through the formality of registration?

## Is Copyright Registration Necessary?

Many benefits do result from registration and substantial detriments can result from failure to register. Moreover, registration is a relatively straightforward and inexpensive process. If registration involved much expense or a complex procedure, then there might be instances in which the owner of a work would not consider it to be of significant enough value to warrant registration. But in most cases, it should be worth the small effort and cost. The potential of the work and its use cannot be predicted, so why not assure yourself of all of the benefits offered by copyright registration? What might appear to be an insignificant work could later catch on and become a real money-maker or professional plum.

Even if your work has not been registered and it eventually becomes valuable, you usually can save many of the rights available under the copyright statute by registering the work as soon as you realize its worth. It is the qualifying "usually" and "many of the rights" that can be critical. Failure to register could be an irrevocable disaster in a limited number of situations. The minimal cost and effort required to avoid such problems usually weighs strongly in favor of registration.

## Benefits of Copyright Registration

Some of the advantages of, or reasons for, copyright registration follow:

1. If your work is registered with the United States Copyright Office, you are entitled to sue in the federal courts anyone who copies, distributes, performs, or otherwise uses your work without your consent. You cannot sue for copyright infringement until your claim to copyright is registered.

2. Copyright registration before someone begins an infringing use of your work is a prerequisite to the recovery of statutory damages and attorney's fees (both of which can be substantial) in an infringement suit. Actual damages and the additional profits of an infringer may be recovered even though registration occurs after the infringement begins. However, failure to register your claim to copyright at an early date may reduce the potential recovery from an infringer to the degree that it makes litigation economically unfeasible.

3. A copyright-registration certificate, when introduced into evidence in litigation, will constitute prima facie evidence of the validity of your copyright and the facts stated in the certificate, if the claim to copyright was registered before or within five years of publication of your work. Thus, you have the advantage of forcing your opponent to overcome the presumption that your rights are valid.

4. Copyright registration can be employed to overcome the omission of the copyright notice from published copies of your work. If you publicly distribute a substantial number of copies without the proper copyright notice, your rights in the work will expire five years from publication unless you register a claim to copyright and place the proper copyright notice on the copies distributed after discovery of the error.

5. Copyright registration will reduce the likelihood of others "innocently" infringing your work as a result of errors or the omission of the copyright notice. If the name in your copyright notice is incorrect—for example, the name of a former copyright owner or the owner of a collective work—your copyright registration will

prohibit the ability of others to deal "innocently" with the person named in the copyright notice.

6. Your application for copyright registration will be reviewed for the proper statutory formalities by the Copyright Office, and it may bring to your attention correctable errors. Correction of errors in the copyright notice at an early date will minimize the likelihood of innocent infringement of your work, as well as total loss of your rights.

7. Copyright registration provides the basis for a permanent, official record of ownership on file with the United States Copyright Office. Moreover, if your work is registered, assignments, licenses, mortgages, and bequests can be recorded in the Copyright Office, and they will be given the effect of constructive notice to others throughout the United States of the rights affected.

8. Copyright registration will entitle you to collect compulsory royalty payments for the use of your musical composition. Musical compositions that have been recorded by the author and have had phonorecords publicly distributed are subject to compulsory licensing. Those persons who make their own recordings of your musical work under the compulsory-licensing provisions must pay you a royalty if you have registered a claim to copyright in the work.

9. Registration of a claim to copyright will entitle you to apply for the importation of foreign-manufactured copies of English-language, nondramatic, literary works. A limited number by an American author, 2,000 copies, can be imported. Registration of a later edition manufactured in the United States also will allow you to correct the previous improper importation of copies.

10. Copyright registration is required in order to renew certain works and thereby increase the term or life of the copyright in these works. Unregistered works published before 1978 and still in their first term of copyright must be registered in order to renew their terms for an additional forty-seven years.

11. Copyright registration also can lead to marketing opportunities. Those who are interested in a particular subject may discover your work through the records of the Copyright Office and contact you regarding possible business opportunities. You may be able to convert a potential infringer into a profitable licensee.

## Best Time to Register

The information regarding the advantages of copyright registration and the effects of failure to register should help you decide *if* you want to register your work. The next question is: *When* is the best time to apply for copyright registration? Prior to the copyright-law revisions effective in 1978, publication was required in order to register a claim to copyright in some kinds of works—most notably, written works. This is no longer true. You can now register claims to copyright at any time you wish in all types of works that are fixed in a tangible medium—prior to publication, at the time of publication, after publication, or even without the intent to ever publish.

**Before completion of the total work.** You may have reason to register your work even before it is completed. For example, you may want to publish part of a manuscript, perhaps to use as a contribution to a magazine; or you may want to circulate it to potential buyers and you may feel more comfortable if the work is registered. You can register a portion of the work, but only the part submitted to the Copyright Office will be covered by the registration. The copyright registered will not cover the unsubmitted part of the work; that portion, when in a tangible form, with copies available to send to the Copyright Office, must be registered separately. Since each finished, tangible piece of an overall work can be the basis for a separate claim to copyright, it is possible to register several separate portions of the overall work that in the end will comprise one, undivided work. Of course, unless you have specific reasons for registering in increments, this could be an expensive and time-consuming effort.

**Before publication.** Usually, a key factor in deciding whether to register an unpublished work is the amount of exposure the work will have to the public before publication. The greater the exposure, the greater will be the risk of the work getting out of your control, in which case, registration prior to publication is a good idea.

Registration prior to publication usually has the additional advantage of requiring only one copy of your work to be deposited.

If the work is registered while in an unpublished form, re-registration after publication is permitted by statute and may be desirable. Re-registration allows the facts (particularly the date of publication) to be recorded in the Copyright Office. The publication date can determine the duration of the copyright in certain types of works. Registration before publication and re-registration after publication naturally mean additional cost and effort.

**Before submitting to a publisher.** If you are dependent upon submitting your work to others, to a publishing company for instance, you may want to register your claim to copyright before the work leaves your control. Registration, however, is not an absolute necessity. Publishing companies, whether for literary, artistic, or musical works, are usually familiar with the copyright laws and are aware of an author's legal right to prevent copying of his or her work even though it is not registered.

**"For hire" works.** If you have been employed to create the work, it will be a work "for hire" and your employer will be the "author" and the only legal registrant or copyright claimant. You should not register the work yourself, even though you may be shown on the copyright application filed by the employer as having been employed to create the work.

**Usual "best" time.** The "best" time to register your work will depend upon your individual circumstances. For most creators of copyrightable works, the best time probably will fall somewhere between completion of the work and a short period after publication. Waiting until completion will avoid the need for multiple registrations of portions of the work. Delaying registration for any substantial period of time after publication usually has little advantage and may cause a significant loss of rights.

Legally, it is possible to wait many years after publication before copyright registration. In fact, you can register your copyright claim any time during the life of your copyright. However, five years from publication should be the longest an author waits to register. Registration after that period of time is usually still possible and should be applied for if, through oversight or other reasons, registration was delayed. More than a five-year delay can cause a permanent loss of rights. If, for example, the proper copyright notice has been omitted from the copies or phonorecords by the copyright owner and a large number of copies have been distributed, the only way to prevent the copyright from being invalidated will be to register the work within five years of publication and to make a reasonable effort to add the notice to the subsequently distributed copies or phonorecords. Moreover, registration before or within five years of publication is required in order to be entitled to a presumption that your copyright is valid.

Registration of your copyright within three months of publication is a good idea. In addition to the advantages of registering within five years, if you register within three months of the date of first publication you will have satisfied the prerequisite for the collection of statutory damages and attorney's fees. Certainly, a very good time to register is no later than three months after first publication of your work.

Perhaps the best rule for timing copyright registration is: when in doubt, register. Loss of rights can result from waiting, and it is seldom worth the risk.

# 2 how to register a claim to copyright

## APPLICATION FORMS AND FEES

Copyright registration is usually a relatively simple procedure that you can do for yourself without an attorney's help. However, since the copyright claim will result in an official record that may be important to you, you should take time to understand what you are doing and to prepare the application accurately.

In order to register your claim to copyright, you must file with the Copyright Office an acceptable application form, the appropriate fee, and a deposit of the required number of copies or phonorecords. The effective date of registration is the day on which these materials are received by the Copyright Office. There are four basic application forms and four additional forms for special situations. All of the application forms are reproduced in this book, as are the instruction sheets attached by the Copyright Office to each form. These forms are included so that you can familiarize yourself with their appearance and content, but you *must* write the Copyright Office for the actual forms. Forms photocopied or taken from this book will not be accepted by the Copyright Office.

## How to Select the Correct Application Form

First, make certain you use the form that is appropriate to your particular work. In some cases, you may have difficulty in deciding which form to use because your work may fall into more than one class. For example, if your work is a book of poetry accompanied by illustrations, you may not know whether to use Form TX (see page 38 ff.), "Application for Copyright Registration for a Nondramatic Literary Work," for the poetry, or Form VA (see page 58 ff.), "Application for a Copyright Registration for a Work of the Visual Arts," for the illustrations. Usually, the best choice is to select the application form for the type of subject that predominates in the work. However, if you have used an inappropriate form, the Copyright Office usually will notify you that in its opinion another form is required and will give you an opportunity to correct your error. Even if you or the Copyright Office should cause the registration to be in the "wrong" class through use of the wrong form, this will not affect any of your rights of copyright ownership.

To assist in selecting the correct forms, what follows is a short description of each classification and the types of works that fall within that class. The list does not cover every possibility because there are so many types of works that can be copyrighted—from sonatas to maps for terrestrial navigation. If you do not find your particular type of work listed here, it does not mean that it is not copyrightable. You should be able to determine the most probable class into which your work falls from its similarity to types of work that are listed. If you still cannot determine which class your work falls into and, accordingly, which form to use, write or call the Copyright Information Office (see page 208 for the address and telephone number).

***Class TX—nondramatic literary works.*** This is a very broad class that includes most types of written work, with the exception of works meant for the performing arts, or in some cases, for audiovisual presentations. Some of the types of work included in this class are:

| | |
|---|---|
| Abridgments | Anthologies |
| Advertising copy | Catalogs |
| Annual publications | Compilations of information |

Contributions to periodicals
Contributions to collective works
Directories
Dissertations
Encyclopedias
Fiction
Instructions
Leaflets
Lectures
Letters
Magazines
Newspapers
Nonfiction
Pamphlets
Periodicals
Poetry
Reference books
Rules of play for games
Sermons
Short stories
Technical writings
Translations

If you are contributing to a collective work, such as a magazine, newspaper, directory, or anthology, you should use the form which applies to the specific type of work that you have created, not the form which would be used to cover the collective work. If, for example, you contribute illustrations to a collection of short stories, you would use Form VA, "Application for Copyright Registration for a Work of the Visual Arts," not Form TX, "Application for Copyright Registration for a Nondramatic Literary Work." The latter form would apply to the book as a whole.

**Class VA—works of the visual arts**. If your work is primarily of a visual nature, either two- or three-dimensional, it will fall into this class. The following types of graphic, pictorial, and sculptural works are included:

Advertising art
Applied art
Architectural designs
Art reproductions
Ceramics
Charts and graphs
Commercial art
Designs
Diagrams
Dolls
Drawings
Enamels
Engineering plans
Filmstrips
Fabric designs
Globes
Greeting cards
Jewelry
Illustrations
Labels
Maps
Models
Paintings
Photographs

| | |
|---|---|
| Picture postcards | Slides |
| Printmaking | Tapestries |
| Scientific renderings | Technical drawings |
| Sculpture | Wallpaper designs |

**Class PA—works of the performing arts.** If your work was created for the purpose of performance before an audience, it should be registered in this class using Form PA, "Application for Copyright Registration for a Work of the Performing Arts" (see page 48 ff.). This applies to works to be performed before a live audience and those works that can be projected to the audience by means of indirect transmission, such as television. Works included are:

| | |
|---|---|
| Audiovisual works | Musical comedies |
| (including the sound track) | Musical compositions |
| Choreography | Operas |
| Dramatic presentations | Pantomimes |
| Motion pictures | Plays |
| (including the sound track) | |

**Class SR—sound recordings.** A somewhat subtle distinction is made between "sound recordings" and "phonorecords" under the Copyright Act. "Sound recording" refers to the creative work, or "writing," and is the subject of copyright protection. The "phonorecord" is simply the physical object in which the sound recording is embodied. Phonorecords may include tapes, records, discs, and other sound-recording media. The work or sound recording which is registered may be a series of musical, spoken, or other sounds, but sound tracks from audiovisual works are specifically excluded and should be registered in class PA. Not all works reproduced on phonorecords (tapes, records, discs) can be registered in class SR. Computer programs, for example, are often reproduced on tape cassettes, but since they do not contain sounds, they fall into class TX, not class SR.

Works that are included in Class SR are:

| | |
|---|---|
| Advertising | Instructional material |
| Comedy | Lectures |
| Dramatic readings | Music |

Poetry                          Sermons
Recitals                        Sound effects

If your work is a sound recording, you usually will have a choice of filing one or two copyright applications. You can register the sound recording and the underlying work (the literary, dramatic, or musical work contained within the sound recording) simultaneously by means of one Form SR application (see page 68 ff.). Alternatively, you can register the sound recording on a Form SR application and the underlying work on a Form TX (see page 38 ff.) or Form PA application (see page 48 ff.)—depending upon the nature of the underlying work. If the copyright claimant of the sound recording is different from the claimant of the underlying work, there is no option; the two works must be registered by separate applications. The copyright protection of the sound recording protects the creativity or authorship involved in presenting or expressing the underlying work in a recorded medium, a phonorecord. The protection given the underlying work extends beyond the particular performance or rendition of the work captured by the sound recording and extends to all uses of the work which are the exclusive right of the copyright owner.

## How to Obtain Application Forms

When you have decided which form to use, write to the Information and Publications Section, Copyright Office, Library of Congress, Washington, D.C. 20559, and request the "Application for Copyright Registration" forms that you need for your particular type of work. Identify the forms either by class—for example, Form TX—or by title—for example, "Application for Copyright Registration for a Nondramatic Literary Work." The forms are free, and if you plan to use a relatively large number for various works, you can request them on a continuous roll without the instruction pages. You *must* use the new forms, which became effective on January 1, 1978. If you have the old forms and send them in for registration, they will not be accepted because they do not contain the information required by the many changes under the revised law. The forms you will receive can be used for either published or unpublished works.

## Fee Schedule

Payment of the copyright registration fee is required before the claim to copyright will be registered. The payment can be in the form of a check, bank draft, or money order in U.S. dollars, made payable to Register of Copyrights. Failure to enclose the fee with the application for registration will delay registration until the fee is received. The registration fee is generally $10 per application, and the following is a schedule of the fees commonly encountered:

1.  Registration fee for all classes: $10 per each registration
2.  Renewal registration fee: $6 each
3.  Fee for additional certificates: $4 each
4.  Fee for recording of documents (such as transfers of ownership): $10 per single document listing one title and consisting of no more than six pages, plus 50 cents for each additional page or title
5.  Fee for recording statements (statement of identity of author of anonymous or pseudonymous work, or statement relating to death of an author): $10 per statement listing one title and consisting of no more than six pages, plus $1 for each additional page or title
6.  Filing notice of intention to make phonorecords: $6
7.  Import Statements fee: $3
8.  Fee for receipt for deposit of copies or phonorecords: $2
9.  Fee for searches: $10 per hour or fraction of an hour for staff to search records

If you use the services of the Copyright Office frequently and want to avoid making many small, individual payments, you can open a deposit account with the Copyright Office from which registration and service fees can be automatically deducted. If you wish to open a deposit account, you should write to the Copyright Office and request the form provided for this purpose. An initial minimum deposit of $250 is required, and all future deposits also must be at least $250. In order to keep the account active, a minimum of twelve transactions a year must be made. You will be given an account number and receive regular statements showing the transaction charges, deposits, and current balance.

When a deposit account is used, transactions will only be made if there are sufficient funds in the account to cover the cost of the fees or services. Therefore, when using such an account, it is very important to make certain that you have enough money in the account to cover all fees to be charged. Otherwise, delays may result that could seriously affect your rights. The Copyright Office will hold your application and notify you that your deposit account has insufficient funds, but if the proper fee is not received in time your rights could be lost. For example, failure to pay a renewal fee on time will result in termination of your copyright.

# DEPOSIT OF COPIES OR PHONORECORDS WITH YOUR APPLICATION FOR REGISTRATION

When you submit an application for copyright registration, you will be required to furnish the Copyright Office with either one or two copies or phonorecords of the work or other "identifying material," depending on the nature of the work and whether or not it has been published.

The term "copies" refers to the material object in which the copyrighted work is fixed; for example, a literary work may be fixed in a book. The literary work is the "writing" which is the subject of copyright. The physical objects, the books, are "copies" and are the means by which the creative expression can be embodied and communicated to others. The term "copies" applies to all types of works—literary, artistic, musical—with the single exception of sound recordings, which are works that are physically embodied in "phonorecords."

The Copyright Office requires that deposits of a work be "complete" copies or phonorecords, and, if the work is published, that the deposit is selected from the "best edition" of the work.

## Complete Copies or Phonorecords

Whether or not your work is published, you must always send the "complete" copy or phonorecord of the work, that is, a copy or phonorecord that contains all of the material for which you are making a claim to copyright. As previously noted, you may register a portion of a larger work. The "complete" copy in this case will be the portion that is being registered. Copyright registration covers only the work as it is represented by the material actually deposited; it does not extend to unfinished portions of the work, nor does it extend to finished portions that are not deposited.

A complete copy will include all elements comprising the work, even though some elements would not be registrable alone or apart from the work. For example, when your work is a contribution to a collective work, such as a magazine article, the "complete" copy of your work is the entire magazine which includes your contribution (for newspapers you need only deposit the entire section that includes your contribution).

A complete phonorecord of a published sound recording includes the phonorecord (record, tape, cassette, and so on) plus any printed matter or visually perceptible material published with the phonorecord, such as textual or pictorial material appearing on a record sleeve or album cover; and any leaflet or booklet included in a sleeve, album, or other container for the phonorecord.

## Best Edition

If your work has been published, you will, in many instances, have to deposit the "best edition" of the work. The Library of Congress has established a "Best Edition Statement," which has criteria for determining which among several published editions will be considered the "best edition" for the purposes of the Library of Congress. This statement is primarily of interest to publishing companies and is not reproduced in this book.

For most authors there will be little debate as to what constitutes the "best edition." Often, there is only one published version, and it will necessarily constitute the best edition; this is true even though the published edition is reproduced by photocopying, mimeographing, or hand lettering. The process of reproduction of the only published edition will not prevent the copies from being the "best edition."

If an edition was first published by distribution of photocopies and later published by offset printing, the offset edition will be the "best edition." Usually, the highest-quality edition will be the best edition. You determine the "best edition" at the time of application for registration. Accordingly, the author need not wait until a printed "better" edition of his work is published. If a photocopied published edition is the only edition that has been published at the time the application for registration is made, deposit of copies of that edition will meet the "best edition" requirements, even though a "better" edition may be published later.

If two editions of your work contain different copyrightable content, they both should be separately registered. One edition is not the "best edition" of the other, even though you may think one edition is an improvement over the other.

When a work exists in more than one medium, for example, in both books and phonorecords, it is preferable to deposit printed matter rather than phonorecords. In the case of newspapers, dissertations, and theses, however, it is preferable to deposit microform (microfilm, microfiche) copies rather than printed copies.

## Preservation of a Duplicate Deposit

Copies and phonorecords deposited with the Copyright Office immediately become the property of the Copyright Office, even if your application is rejected and returned. The Copyright Office has complete discretion as to whether or not to retain or dispose of your copies or phonorecords. Most deposits are kept for several years, but eventually sheer volume requires the destruction of deposits. If your work is unpublished, the Copyright Office must, however, make a facsimile reproduction before destroying the deposit. No such facsimile is required before destruction of published works. It is also possible for a copyright owner to specifically request that the Copyright Office retain the deposit for the life of the copyright. Such a request will require payment of an additional fee beyond the application fee.

The copyright owner should, therefore, keep an exact copy of the work he or she has deposited with the Copyright Office. *Do not automatically rely upon the copy deposited with the Copyright Office as a permanent record of your work.* Even works that now would have become collector's items have been destroyed. Charles Darrow's first set of rules for the game "Monopoly" has, for example, been destroyed.

If you become involved in litigation in connection with your work, you may have to prove exactly what was deposited with the Copyright Office without being able to obtain a certified copy from the Copyright Office. One way of doing this is to keep a witnessed duplicate copy in your own files. When you are about to send your application for copyright registration to the Copyright Office, have a witness, or preferably two witnesses, compare the copies to be deposited with a duplicate copy that you intend to keep. The witness should sign and date your duplicate copy and indicate that it is identical to the copies forwarded to the Copyright Office.


## Deposit to Accompany Application

The application, fee, and deposit should be forwarded together to the Copyright Office. However, if for some reason you need to mail the deposit separately from the application and fee, you should enclose a letter with the application stating that the deposit is coming separately and that the enclosed application should be held for receipt of that deposit. And you should enclose a letter with the deposit identifying it as belonging with the separately forwarded application. If you don't indicate that the deposit is to be used with a specific application for copyright registration, the Copyright Office will treat it as a deposit for the Library of Congress, which will *not* satisfy the deposit requirements for copyright registration.

The Library of Congress is authorized and empowered to require deposit of copies of all works published in the United States, and while this deposit requirement is similar to the copyright registration deposit requirement, they are not the same. Deposit of copies or phonorecords with the copyright application will simultaneously satisfy the registration and Library of Congress deposit requirements, but deposit of copies or phonorecords without reference to an application for copyright registration will satisfy only the Library of Congress deposit requirement.

# Deposit Requirements for Classes TX, PA, VA, and SR

The number of copies or phonorecords to be deposited with your application for copyright registration are governed by the following general rules:

1. Unpublished Works—one complete copy or phonorecord
2. Works First Published before January 1, 1978—two complete copies or phonorecords of the work as first published
3. Works First Published after January 1, 1978—two complete copies or phonorecords of the best edition
4. Works First Published Outside the United States—one complete copy or phonorecord as published
5. Contributions to Collective Works—one complete copy or phonorecord of the best edition of the collective work

## Exceptions to Standard Requirements

In addition, the Copyright Office has established exceptions to the general rules that depend upon the nature of the work. These exceptions are explained as follows according to the class in which the work falls. If you find that your work presents an *unusual* deposit problem, you can contact the Copyright Office and discuss the problem.

***All classes—works that exceed ninety-six inches in any dimension.*** If the deposit of a copy or phonorecord will exceed ninety-six inches in any dimension, you must submit "identifying material" instead of copies. The types of identifying material required are usually photographic reproductions in the form of prints (preferably 8 × 10 inches), transparencies (35 millimeter), or photostats. Drawings and renderings can also be used. The identifying reproductions of the work must include *all* of the copyrightable subject matter. Therefore, several pictorial representations may be necessary to show the complete work—for example, all sides of a three-dimensional work. Reproductions must also show the form and location of the copyright notice, if the work has been published. In addition, the identifying reproductions of the work preferably should be its actual size, although it may be necessary to use enlargements to show the copyright notice or reductions to show the entire work. The dimension of the work should be indicated on the back side of the photograph.

**Class TX—nondramatic literary works.** Most nondramatic literary works follow the general deposit rules. One complete copy should be deposited with your application for unpublished works and two complete copies of the best edition for published works. Similarly, one copy is deposited if the work is first published outside the United States; as is one complete copy of the collective work, if your work is a contribution to a collective work.

There are some exceptions. The Copyright Office will accept *one* copy of the best edition of a nondramatic literary work instead of the *two* normally required in the following instances: (1) Lectures, sermons, speeches, and addresses published individually and not as part of a collection; and (2) tests and answers published separately from other literary works. (Arrangements can be made for the return of "secure tests" which are deposited.)

It should be noted that delivery of a speech, lecture, or sermon—even to a very large audience—is not a publication of the speech; there must be a public distribution of copies of the speech. If copies of a speech are publicly distributed, then the speech is published, but only a single copy need be deposited with the Copyright Office.

Additionally, if the literary work is fixed or published in a machine-readable form only, such as computer programs and data bases, the Copyright regulations require the deposit of one copy of "identifying portions," instead of copies, of the machine-readable materials themselves. If you are faced with this problem, you should contact the Copyright Office as to the definition of "identifying portions" for computer programs and data bases.

**Class VA—works of the visual arts.** While most nondramatic literary works follow the general deposit rules, most works in the visual arts do not. The general rules (two copies for published works and one for unpublished works) still apply, but the inherent nature of many works of the visual arts compels numerous exceptions. For example, deposit of even one copy of a work of fine art might cause the artist to forsake copyright registration because there may only be one existing copy, the original.

One complete copy of the best edition of the following published works of the visual arts will be accepted instead of the usual requirement of two:

1. Three-dimensional cartographic representations of areas, such as globes and relief maps or models
2. Diagrams illustrating technical or scientific information
3. Architectural or engineering blueprints and mechanical drawings
4. ·Greeting cards, picture postcards, and stationery
5. Prints, labels, and other advertising material published in connection with the sale or lease of articles of merchandise, works of authorship, or services (one copy of the entire page of periodicals or the like in which the work appears)
6. Textiles, fabrics, wallpaper, carpeting, floor tile, floor coverings, wrapping paper, and similar works published only in the form of two-dimensional reproductions on sheetlike material. (An actual swatch showing the design and copyright notice, and if it repeats, at least one repetition of the design)

Graphic or pictorial works that are unpublished or published in small numbers or limited editions do not require deposit of even one copy. Instead, identifying photographic material or drawings may be deposited, although the author may *elect* to deposit one copy of the work instead of "identifying material." To qualify, a published graphic or pictorial work must have had less than five copies published, or the work must have been published in a limited edition of no more than 300 numbered copies.

If the work of the visual arts is a three-dimensional work or is embodied in or affixed to a three-dimensional work, "identifying material"—photographic or graphic reproductions—can be deposited in the place of a copy or copies. Examples are prints and labels that are inseparable from a three-dimensional object, fabrics published only as wearing apparel or in furniture, sculptural works, carvings, ceramics, jewelry, dolls, toys, games, and three-dimensional useful articles including copyrightable material.

**Class PA—works of the performing arts.** Again, the standard rules of one complete copy for unpublished works and two complete copies of the best edition for published works apply to works of the performing arts. As in the case of the visual arts, however, there are numerous exceptions to the general deposit requirements. These exceptions have been created to accommodate practical problems that would arise if the general requirements were strictly followed.

One complete copy of the best edition will be accepted instead of the two copies usually required in the following instances: (1) musical compositions published only by the rental, lease, or lending of copies; (2) published multimedia kits used for systematic instructional activities and including literary works, audiovisual works, sound recordings, or any combination of such works; (3) published motion pictures. The deposit must be accompanied by a separate description of the contents, such as a synopsis.

Additionally, the deposit requirement for unpublished motion pictures can be satisfied by the deposit of identifying material. Identifying material in this case is comprised of a description of the motion picture *plus* either an audio cassette or other phonorecord of the sound track, *or* a set of one-frame enlargements taken from each ten-minute segment of the motion picture. There is also an exception to the general deposit requirements for sound tracks that are integral parts of motion pictures. Instead of the sound track, a copy or copies of a phonorecord reproduction of the entire work *and* photographs showing the title, sound track credits, and copyright notice, if any, will suffice.

**Class SR—sound recordings.** Sound recordings follow the general deposit requirements of one complete phonorecord for unpublished works and two complete phonorecords of the best edition for published works. The primary deviation from these rules is that for published sound recordings a complete phonorecord of the best edition also must include any visually perceptible material published with the phonorecord. Thus, written and pictorial matter appearing on record sleeves or album covers, or in leaflets or booklets contained in a sleeve, album, or phonorecord container must also be deposited.

As explained in the description of works in class SR, "sound recording" and "phonorecord" do not mean the same thing. A sound recording is the creative act of fixation of sounds expressing an underlying work on a tangible recording medium. The medium in which the sounds are fixed is the "phonorecord," a generic term that applies to tapes or cassettes as well as records. Thus, a "sound recording" is fixed in a "phonorecord," just as a literary work is tangibly fixed in a "copy."

Since there are often two works contained in a phonorecord—the sound recording and the underlying work—you usually have the choice of filing one or two copyright registrations, and, accordingly, a choice with regard to the copyright deposit.

First, you may apply for registration of both works—the sound recording and underlying musical, dramatic, or literary work—in the same application, if the copyright claimant or claimants are the same in both works. If you do this, you should use Form SR, "Application for Copyright Registration for a Sound Recording" (see page 68 ff.), and deposit a single phonorecord for unpublished works and two phonorecords, including accompanying materials, for published works. This deposit will suffice for registration of *both* the underlying work and the sound recording.

Second, if you do not want to or cannot register a claim to copyright in the sound recording, you may register just the dramatic, literary, or musical work. Use Form PA if your work is a work of the performing arts, or Form TX if your work is a nondramatic literary work. You can deposit phonorecords if no published written copies exist, but if there are copies, then the "best edition" will be published copies rather than the published phonorecords. You must deposit published copies if they are available.

Third, you may also elect to make two separate applications for registration of the sound recording and the underlying work. Use Form SR for the sound recording and deposit one phonorecord for unpublished works or two phonorecords for published works. For the underlying dramatic, musical, or literary work, use Form PA or Form TX and deposit phonorecords or, if available, copies of the work. In the event that the copyright claimant is different for the sound recording and the underlying dramatic, musical, or literary work, two separate applications must be filed.

# HOW TO COMPLETE THE APPLICATION FOR COPYRIGHT REGISTRATION FOR NONDRAMATIC LITERARY WORKS, WORKS OF THE PERFORMING ARTS, WORKS OF THE VISUAL ARTS, SOUND RECORDINGS

When you write to the Copyright Office for an application form for registration of a claim to copyright, you will also receive instructions on how to fill out each form. All of the forms and instructions are reprinted in this book. Most of the instructions are explicit and easy to grasp; but the following additional information may be helpful in filling out the forms. In any case, read the instructions on each form carefully.

Since the questions in each of the four basic copyright application forms are almost identical, they are explained together. Read this explanation regardless of which form you are using. Whenever a comment is relevant to only one particular form, this variance is noted. The following general information applies to the four basic application forms: Form TX (Nondramatic Literary Works), Form PA (Works of the Performing Arts), Form VA (Works of the Visual Arts), Form SR (Sound Recording).

## Title of Work—Space 1 on Forms TX, PA, VA, and SR

Even if your work is untitled, you nevertheless must give it an identifying title for the purpose of registration. For example, an untitled painting might be identified as "Watercolor Series No. 5—1979." Put this phrase in the "Title" space of the application. Also, make certain that you note in your own permanent records the title that you have used in the registration form. If the work has been identified by other titles prior to the first application for registration, enter those titles under "Previous or Alternative Titles."

If your work has an identifying title, it may be helpful to add parenthetically a short descriptive expression. For example, you may want to register a claim to copyright for a series of similar advertisements. Each advertisement may bear the trademark of the product at the top, and the trademark can be used as the title in the copyright application. Thus, if the mark is "ACME PRODUCTS" you might want to use the title "ACME PRODUCTS (Hand Tools)." This will help identify and distinguish the registration from similar registrations for other advertisements in the series, for example, another advertisement could be titled, "ACME PRODUCTS (Power Tools)." If the work has a title that clearly identifies it, simply use that title. If the work has a subtitle on it that would help identify the work, you can use the subtitle. If no subtitle is present, you should add one only if necessary or helpful in identifying the work.

You should not use the "Title" section to "tell your story," and any parenthetical material added should serve to identify the work, not describe its contents or merit. Added material that does not appear on the copies of the work itself will be closely examined by the Copyright Office·to determine whether or not it is helpful in identifying the work.

## Name of Author—Space 2 on Forms TX, PA, VA, and SR

Each person contributing to the creation of the copyright work must be listed as an author. This is required even though some of the authors or contributors may not be claiming copyright ownership. For example, you may want to donate a chapter to a book simply because you wish to have certain information made available to the public. You may have no interest in any personal benefits to be derived from copyright ownership, but you should nonetheless be listed as an author. Your name would not appear in the copyright notice upon publication of the work, nor would it appear in space 4 of the registration form for copyright "Claimant(s)," but it must be included in space 2 of the application under "Author(s)."

**Works made "for hire."** The Copyright Office instruction sheet briefly describes "works made for hire," and a more detailed description is contained in Chapter 5 of this book. If you are seeking to register a work made for hire, the author is the employer, not the person who was hired to prepare the work. You should list the full legal name of the employer; do not guess about the full legal name. Showing the employer as "ABC, Inc.," when in fact its full legal name is "ABC Incorporated" or "ABC Company, Inc.," will create an ambiguity in title that probably will have to be corrected at a later date.

**Collective works.** If the work is a contribution to a collective work, the author is the contributing party. If the work being registered is the collective work, the author is the person(s) or organization responsible for the collection. It is not necessary to show individual authors of the contributions to the collective work as "authors" of the collective work—they created the contributions, not the collection of contributions.

**Anonymous and pseudonymous works.** Anonymous work means that no name of an author appears on the copies or phonorecords.

Pseudonymous work means that a fictitious name appears on the copies or phonorecords as the author, rather than the author's own name.

Before you decide to use a pseudonym or publish anonymously, consider whether your purpose is sufficiently important to risk the possible complications. Although it might be fun to have one or more pen names, unless you have a serious or unusual reason for assuming another name, it would be best to avoid the legal complexities that can arise from the use of such pseudonyms. The same also will be true for anonymous works. You should see a copyright attorney if you wish to register an anonymous or pseudonymous work so that the relationship between you, as author, and the copyright claimant can be documented and properly reflected on the records of the Copyright Office.

**Nature of authorship.** The nature of authorship requires only a brief description. Limit this to a general statement of the nature of your creativity; do not give a detailed account of your contribution or list each page you wrote. You can simply indicate "author of text" or "author of illustrations and some portions of text."

Occasionally, the Copyright Office will challenge your statement of the nature of authorship. For example, use of the statement, "artwork and text" on an application for a greeting card having a short saying or phrase, such as "keep on smiling," will probably raise objections on the basis that the "text"—the saying or phrase—is not long or material enough to constitute a work of copyrightable authorship. You should describe the nature of the authorship in such a greeting card merely as "artwork." If you have included a poem on the card, however, you should describe the nature of the authorship as "artwork and text."

## Creation and Publication—Space 3 on TX, PA, VA, and SR

Creation of a work occurs when it is first fixed in a tangible medium, either copies or phonorecords. You need only give the year of creation, not the exact date. You should not use the year you first thought of the idea; the idea must be expressed by fixation in a tangible medium. You can register a claim to copyright to a part of your work before the entire work is completed, in which case the date of creation is the year the part of the work being registered was finished.

Date of first publication is the date when copies or phonorecords were distributed to the public by sale, other transfer of ownership, or rental. Additionally, publication will occur upon the offering of copies or phonorecords to others for their distribution, public performance, or display. If the author has merely displayed or publicly performed the work himself, this will not, under the new copyright law, constitute publication.

The exact date of first publication, not merely the year, is required for published works. If the exact date is unknown, the first day of the month in which publication occurred can be used.

## Copyright Claimants—Space 4 on Forms TX, PA, VA, and SR

*Claimants and authors.* The people or organizations who should be listed in this space are those who are claiming ownership of the copyright. They are not necessarily the same as the authors. Upon creation of a work, the author is always the copyright owner, but very often the author will have transferred copyright ownership to another person or organization before registration takes place. At the time of registration, a person may be an author without being a claimant, and a claimant need not be an author. Do not automatically fill in the same names here as in space 2. List only those people who are the actual copyright owners.

*Joint ownership.* In the case of joint authorship, do not select one person as the claimant to represent the other people. The claimant is not a representative acting on behalf of a group. Each person with an ownership interest in the property should be listed here.

*Work made "for hire."* If the work was prepared "for hire," list the party for whom the work was prepared as the claimant since that party is the owner of the work. It is possible that the employer has subsequently transferred the work to another and would no longer be the claimant, but generally an application for a "work made for hire" will show the employer as both author and claimant.

*Transfers.* If the rights to the work have been transferred prior to registration and the author is no longer the copyright owner, list the name of the new owner and briefly explain the means of transfer, for example, "assigned on January 15, 1979, to ABC Publisher." Any time a person or entity other than the author is shown as the claimant, an explanation must be entered in the "Transfer" portion of space 4.

Transfers of copyright ownership are not valid unless contained in a written document signed by the owner transferring the rights; merely showing the transfer on the application for registration is not sufficient.

**Anonymous and pseudonymous works.** If the work is anonymous or pseudonymous a copyright claimant still must be listed. You can show the real name of the author under the claimant or even go further and state under claimant, "Mr. A. B. Smith pseudonym for M. N. Jones." Copyright registrations are available to the public, however, so if you do not want to reveal your identity on a public record, you must arrange with an agent or other representative to act as claimant. Because of the legal problems this situation could create, consultation with a copyright attorney should be obtained prior to making this decision.

## Previous Registration—Space 5 on Forms TX, PA, VA, and SR

The purpose of this space, in part, is to enable the Copyright Office to determine whether the application for copyright registration is necessary or appropriate. The following are guidelines for deciding if a work should be registered:

1. You should not register a work each time it is printed in the same version. Your original registration will protect all printings of the same copyrighted material. However, if you have changed the work in a way that adds or creates new copyrightable material, you should file a new application for registration to protect the new or "derivative" work that has resulted. It may be difficult to draw the line between insignificant changes, such as punctuation and minor editorial revisions, and changes that result in the creation of new copyrightable subject matter. As a general rule, however, you should apply for registration if you think the additions or changes may include sufficient originality to be copyrightable.

2. You should not register a work again on forms TX, VA, PA, or SR in order to correct errors that were made in filling out an earlier application form. You should file an "Application for Supplementary Copyright Registration" on Form CA to correct errors. Form CA is discussed separately on pages 79 and 86.

3. You should not use forms TX, VA, PA, or SR for renewal of a copyright registration. Use Form RE, "Application for Renewal Registration," which is discussed on pages 111 to 114.

4. Do not use forms TX, VA, PA, or SR to record transfers of copyright ownership. Space 4 is provided to indicate transfers between the author and the claimant before registration, but after the registration has been filed, subsequent transfers are recorded by sending the document of assignment or other transfer to the Copyright Office.

You should register the *same* work again only (1) if the work was previously registered in an unpublished form and is now published; (2) if the work was registered previously with someone other than the author shown as the copyright claimant, and the author now wants to be shown as the claimant in the registration (for example, if someone registers a claim to copyright in your work without your consent); or (3) if the first registration omitted a joint author as a claimant.

Since these last two situations often involve disputes as to ownership, they should not be undertaken lightly and advice from a lawyer is suggested.

An employee who writes or creates a work made "for hire" cannot re-register the same work in her or his own name, since the employee was not the "author"—the employer was.

An additional function of space 5 is to enable new versions or derivative works to be related to the original upon which they are based. When you have a new version with new copyrightable subject matter, the new version should be registered. This registration of the new version is not a re-registration of the original work, but space 5 can be used to cross-reference the original work. The cross-reference enables others to compare the two versions and determine exactly what was added to the new version; this can be particularly important when the copyright on the original work expires.

## Compilations and Derivative Works—Space 6 of Forms TX, PA, VA, and SR

If you have changed an earlier version of your work by adding new material, revising, or rearranging, and if the change warrants a new copyright, you should follow the instructions for derivative works. Sometimes, there are questions as to whether or not the changes constitute copyrightable authorship. As has been indicated, it is best to file a new registration if you are in doubt. In some instances, changes will clearly be stenographic in nature. Re-registration would not be necessary since stenographic changes do not affect copyright protection in the work. Other changes may only amount to reorganization of existing material, but the reorganization may add materially to the overall impact of the work and would constitute copyrightable subject matter. Space 6 is provided so that you can clearly identify the preexisting material and the nature of the material added or rearranged.

## Manufacturing Requirements—Space 7 on Form TX (Only)

Importation into or public distribution in the United States of a work by an American consisting mainly of nondramatic literary material in the English language is prohibited under the Copyright Act unless the work was manufactured in the United States or Canada. Therefore, if your work is unpublished or not in the English language, you do not need to complete space 7. Exceptions to the manufacturing requirements are discussed on page 87.

You may import 2,000 copies of a nondramatic literary work, if you have obtained an "Import Statement" discussed on page 87. Even if you do not have an Import Statement and the copies were not lawfully manufactured and imported, this will not prevent copyright registration, but your copyright will not be enforceable against others until you register an authorized edition of the work that complies with the manufacturing requirements.

List the name of the manufacturer and the place of manufacture, whether or not the work was manufactured in the United States or Canada, and whether or not an Import Statement has been issued.

## License for Handicapped—Space 8 on Form TX (Only)

If you would like to make your work available to blind or physically handicapped people, complete space 8. The Library of Congress has a special program designed to reproduce and distribute nondramatic literary works that have been published and are adaptable to Braille and/or sound recordings. However, they cannot use your work without your permission. If you want to grant a nonexclusive license for the reproduction and distribution of your work to the blind and physically handicapped, this can be easily done in conjunction with the registration for copyright. Simply check the appropriate boxes in space 8. This nonexclusive license will not prevent you from entering into other licensing agreements.

Also, you may terminate the license at any time; termination will become effective ninety days after notice. The Library of Congress will then be prohibited from reproducing any more copies or phonorecords; however, it may distribute the remaining copies or phonorecords already produced. If the license is not terminated, it will last for the life of the copyright.

## Fee and Correspondence—Space 9 on Form TX and Space 7 on Forms VA, PA, and SR

Your claim to copyright will not be registered until the $10 registration fee is received. The fee may be paid by personal check, money order, or bank draft payable to Register of Copyrights. Do not send currency.

List only one person to whom correspondence can be directed. The person listed need not be the author or claimant. When you are represented by counsel, usually that person is designated to receive correspondence. If the Copyright Office has any objections or questions concerning the application, deposit, or fee, the person designated for correspondence will receive the communications from the Copyright Office.

## Certification—Space 10 on Form TX and Space 8 on Forms VA, PA, and SR

The application for registration of a claim to copyright must be signed and dated. The author, claimant, or owner of an exclusive right (for example, the right to perform the work) can sign the application. Additionally, any of these parties can authorize an agent, such as an attorney, to sign the application. The person signing the application is certifying that the statements made therein are correct to the best of his or her knowledge. Persons knowingly making false statements are subject to a fine of up to $2,500.

## Address for Return of Certificate—Space 11 on Form TX and Space 9 on Forms VA, PA, and SR

The registration certificate that you will receive is simply a photocopy of the application form to which the seal of the Copyright Office, the registration number, and effective date of registration are added. The registration number assigned by the Copyright Office to an unpublished work will include a *u* after the class designation, for example, TXu 4141. Only one certificate will be issued for the basic $10 application fee. If you want additional certificates, an additional fee of $4 for each certificate should be forwarded to the Copyright Office with the application. All of the .certificates will be sent to you at one address.

# COPYRIGHT REGISTRATION FOR A GROUP OF RELATED WORKS

The new Copyright Act authorizes the Copyright Office to adopt regulations that would permit a single copyright registration for any group of related works. As of the publication of this book, however, the Copyright Office has not established regulations implementing such group registrations.

## Works That Qualify

The new act also provides that the Copyright Office "shall" adopt regulations specifically providing for registration of a group of contributions to periodicals. These regulations have been adopted and are now in effect.

# FORM TX

UNITED STATES COPYRIGHT OFFICE
LIBRARY OF CONGRESS
WASHINGTON, D.C. 20559

# APPLICATION
# FOR
# COPYRIGHT
# REGISTRATION
*for a*
*Nondramatic Literary Work*

---

## HOW TO APPLY FOR COPYRIGHT REGISTRATION:

- *First:* Read the information on this page to make sure Form TX is the correct application for your work.

- *Second:* Open out the form by lifting on the left. Read through the detailed instructions before starting to complete the form.

- *Third:* Complete spaces 1-4 of the application, then turn the entire form over and, after reading the instructions for spaces 5-11, complete the rest of your application. Use typewriter or print in dark ink. Be sure to sign the form at space 10.

- **Fourth:** Detach your completed application from these instructions and send it with the necessary deposit of the work (see below) to: Register of Copyrights, Library of Congress, Washington, D.C. 20559. Unless you have a Deposit Account in the Copyright Office, your application and deposit must be accompanied by a check or money order for $10, payable to: *Register of Copyrights.*

**WHEN TO USE FORM TX:** Form TX is the appropriate application to use for copyright registration covering nondramatic literary works, whether published or unpublished.

**WHAT IS A "NONDRAMATIC LITERARY WORK?"** The category of "nondramatic literary works" (Class TX) is very broad. Except for dramatic works and certain kinds of audiovisual works, Class TX includes all types of works written in words (or other verbal or numerical symbols). A few of the many examples of "nondramatic literary works" include fiction, nonfiction, poetry, periodicals, textbooks, reference works, directories, catalogs, advertising copy, and compilations of information.

**DEPOSIT TO ACCOMPANY APPLICATION:** An application for copyright registration must be accompanied by a deposit representing the entire work for which registration is to be made. The following are the general deposit requirements as set forth in the statute:

*Unpublished work:* Deposit one complete copy (or phonorecord).

*Published work:* Deposit two complete copies (or phonorecords) of the best edition.

*Work first published outside the United States:* Deposit one complete copy (or phonorecord) of the first foreign edition.

*Contribution to a collective work:* Deposit one complete copy (or phonorecord) of the best edition of the collective work.

These general deposit requirements may vary in particular situations. For further information about copyright deposit, write for Circular R7.

**THE COPYRIGHT NOTICE:** For published works, the law provides that a copyright notice in a specified form "shall be placed on all publicly distributed copies from which the work can be visually perceived."Use of the copyright notice is the responsibility of the copyright owner and does not require advance permission from the Copyright Office. The required form of the notice for copies generally consists of three elements: (1) the symbol "©", or the word "Copyright", or the abbreviation "Copr."; (2) the year of first publication; and (3) the name of the owner of copyright. For example: "© 1978 Constance Porter". The notice is to be affixed to the copies "in such manner and location as to give reasonable notice of the claim of copyright." Unlike the law in effect before 1978, the new copyright statute provides procedures for correcting errors in the copyright notice, and even for curing the omission of the notice. However, a failure to comply with the notice requirements may still result in the loss of some copyright protection and, unless corrected within five years, in the complete loss of copyright. For further information about the copyright notice and the procedures for correcting errors or omissions, write for Circular R3.

**DURATION OF COPYRIGHT:** For works that were created after the effective date of the new statute (January 1, 1978), the basic copyright term will be the life of the author and fifty years after the author's death. For works made for hire, and for certain anonymous and pseudonymous works, the duration of copyright will be 75 years from publication or 100 years from creation, whichever is shorter. These same terms of copyright will generally apply to works that had been created before 1978 but had not been published or copyrighted before that date. For further information about the duration of copyright, including the terms of copyrights already in existence before 1978, write for Circular R15a.

# FORM TX

UNITED STATES COPYRIGHT OFFICE

REGISTRATION NUMBER

TX            TXU

EFFECTIVE DATE OF REGISTRATION

Month          Day          Year

---

**DO NOT WRITE ABOVE THIS LINE. IF YOU NEED MORE SPACE, USE CONTINUATION SHEET**

**(1) Title**

**TITLE OF THIS WORK:**

**PREVIOUS OR ALTERNATIVE TITLES:**

If a periodical or serial give: Vol....... No....... Issue Date .........

**PUBLICATION AS A CONTRIBUTION:** (If this work was published as a contribution to a periodical, serial, or collection, give information about the collective work in which the contribution appeared.)

Title of Collective Work: ......... Vol....... No....... Date ......... Pages.........

**(2) Author(s)**

**IMPORTANT:** Under the law, the "author" of a "work made for hire" is generally the employer, not the employee (see instructions). If any part of this work was "made for hire" check "Yes" in the space provided, give the employer (or other person for whom the work was prepared) as "Author" of that part, and leave the space for dates blank.

**1**

**NAME OF AUTHOR:**

**DATES OF BIRTH AND DEATH:**

Born ......... Died ......... (Year) (Year)

Was this author's contribution to the work a "work made for hire"?    Yes.......    No.......

**AUTHOR'S NATIONALITY OR DOMICILE:**

Citizen of ......... } or { Domiciled in ......... (Name of Country)                    (Name of Country)

**AUTHOR OF:** (Briefly describe nature of this author's contribution)

**WAS THIS AUTHOR'S CONTRIBUTION TO THE WORK:**

Anonymous?    Yes.......    No.......
Pseudonymous?    Yes.......    No.......

If the answer to either of these questions is "Yes," see detailed instructions attached.

**2**

| NAME OF AUTHOR: | DATES OF BIRTH AND DEATH: |
| --- | --- |
| | Born.......... Died.......... (Year) (Year) |

Was this author's contribution to the work a "work made for hire"?   Yes....... No......

**AUTHOR'S NATIONALITY OR DOMICILE:**

Citizen of .............. } or { Domiciled in .............. (Name of Country) (Name of Country)

**AUTHOR OF:** (Briefly describe nature of this author's contribution)

**WAS THIS AUTHOR'S CONTRIBUTION TO THE WORK:**

Anonymous?   Yes ...... No ......
Pseudonymous?   Yes ...... No ......

If the answer to either of these questions is "Yes," see detailed instructions attached.

**3**

| NAME OF AUTHOR: | DATES OF BIRTH AND DEATH: |
| --- | --- |
| | Born.......... Died.......... (Year) (Year) |

Was this author's contribution to the work a "work made for hire"?   Yes....... No......

**AUTHOR'S NATIONALITY OR DOMICILE:**

Citizen of .............. } or { Domiciled in .............. (Name of Country) (Name of Country)

**AUTHOR OF:** (Briefly describe nature of this author's contribution)

**WAS THIS AUTHOR'S CONTRIBUTION TO THE WORK:**

Anonymous?   Yes ...... No ......
Pseudonymous?   Yes ...... No ......

If the answer to either of these questions is "Yes," see detailed instructions attached.

---

**(3) Creation and Publication**

**YEAR IN WHICH CREATION OF THIS WORK WAS COMPLETED:**

Year............

(This information must be given in all cases.)

**DATE AND NATION OF FIRST PUBLICATION:**

Date.................. ..............
(Month)  (Day)  (Year)

Nation..................
(Name of Country)

(Complete this block ONLY if this work has been published.)

---

**(4) Claimant(s)**

**NAME(S) AND ADDRESS(ES) OF COPYRIGHT CLAIMANT(S):**

**TRANSFER:** (If the copyright claimant(s) named here in space 4 are different from the author(s) named in space 2, give a brief statement of how the claimant(s) obtained ownership of the copyright.)

---

• Complete all applicable spaces (numbers 5-11) on the reverse side of this page
• Follow detailed instructions attached
• Sign the form at line 10

**DO NOT WRITE HERE**

Page 1 of ........ pages

| | EXAMINED BY: .......... | APPLICATION RECEIVED: |
| --- | --- | --- |
| | CHECKED BY: .......... | |
| FOR COPYRIGHT OFFICE USE ONLY | CORRESPONDENCE: ☐ Yes | DEPOSIT RECEIVED: |
| | DEPOSIT ACCOUNT FUNDS USED: ☐ | REMITTANCE NUMBER AND DATE |

**DO NOT WRITE ABOVE THIS LINE. IF YOU NEED ADDITIONAL SPACE, USE CONTINUATION SHEET (FORM TX/CON)**

**PREVIOUS REGISTRATION:**

- Has registration for this work, or for an earlier version of this work, already been made in the Copyright Office?    Yes ......... No .........
- If your answer is "Yes," why is another registration being sought? (Check appropriate box)
  - ☐ This is the first published edition of a work previously registered in unpublished form.
  - ☐ This is the first application submitted by this author as copyright claimant.
  - ☐ This is a changed version of the work, as shown by line 6 of this application.
- If your answer is "Yes," give: Previous Registration Number ..................    Year of Registration ..................

**(5) Previous Registration**

**COMPILATION OR DERIVATIVE WORK:** (See instructions)

PREEXISTING MATERIAL: (Identify any preexisting work or works that this work is based on or incorporates.)

{ ...........................................................................

...........................................................................

MATERIAL ADDED TO THIS WORK: (Give a brief, general statement of the material that has been added to this work and in which copyright is claimed.)

{ ...........................................................................

...........................................................................

**(6) Compilation or Derivative Work**

**MANUFACTURERS AND LOCATIONS:** (If this is a published work consisting preponderantly of nondramatic literary material in English, the law may require that the copies be manufactured in the United States or Canada for full protection. If so, the names of the manufacturers who performed certain processes, and the places where these processes were performed *must* be given. See instructions for details.)

| NAMES OF MANUFACTURERS | PLACES OF MANUFACTURE |
| --- | --- |
| .......................... | .......................... |
| .......................... | .......................... |

**(7) Manufacturing**

/ 43

# REPRODUCTION FOR USE OF BLIND OR PHYSICALLY-HANDICAPPED PERSONS: (See instructions)

• Signature of this form at space 10, and a check in one of the boxes here in space 8, constitutes a non-exclusive grant of permission to the Library of Congress to reproduce and distribute solely for the blind and physically handicapped and under the conditions and limitations prescribed by the regulations of the Copyright Office: (1) copies of the work identified in space 1 of this application in Braille (or similar tactile symbols); or (2) phonorecords embodying a fixation of a reading of that work; or (3) both.

a ☐ Copies and phonorecords    b ☐ Copies Only    c ☐ Phonorecords Only

**(8) License For Handicapped**

---

**DEPOSIT ACCOUNT:** (If the registration fee is to be charged to a Deposit Account established in the Copyright Office, give name and number of Account.)

Name: . . . . . . . . . . . . . . . . . . . . . . . . . . . . . . . . . . . . . . . . . . . . . . . .

Account Number: . . . . . . . . . . . . . . . . . . . . . . . . . . . . . . . . . . . . . . . . . .

**CORRESPONDENCE:** (Give name and address to which correspondence about this application should be sent.)

Name: . . . . . . . . . . . . . . . . . . . . . . . . . . . . . . . . . . . . . . . . . . . . . . . . . . . .

Address: . . . . . . . . . . . . . . . . . . . . . . . . . . . . . . . . . . . . . . . (Apt.)

. . . . . . . . . . . . . . . . . (City) . . . . . . . . . . . (State) . . . . . . . . . . . (ZIP)

**(9) Fee and Correspondence**

---

**CERTIFICATION: ✱** I, the undersigned, hereby certify that I am the: (Check one)

☐ author ☐ other copyright claimant ☐ owner of exclusive right(s) ☐ authorized agent of: . . . . . . . . . . (Name of author or other copyright claimant, or owner of exclusive right(s))

of the work identified in this application and that the statements made by me in this application are correct to the best of my knowledge.

Handwritten signature: (X) . . . . . . . . . . . . . . . . . . . . . . . . . . . . . . . . . . . . . . . . . . . . . . . Date . . . . . . . . .

Typed or printed name. . . . . . . . . . . . . . . . . . . . . . . . . . . . . . . . . . .

**(10) Certification (Application must be signed)**

---

**MAIL CERTIFICATE TO**

*(Certificate will be mailed in window envelope)*

. . . . . . . . . . . . . . . . . . . . . . . . . . . . . . . . . . . . . . . .

. . . . . . . . . . . . . . . . . . . . . . . . . . . . . . . . . . . . . . . .
(Name)

. . . . . . . . . . . . . . . . . . . . . . . . . . . . . . . . . . . . . . . .
(Number, Street and Apartment Number)

. . . . . . . . . . . . . . . . . . . . . . . . . . . . . . . . . . . . . . . .
(City) (State) (ZIP code)

**(11) Address For Return of Certificate**

---

✱ 17 U.S.C. § 506(e): Any person who knowingly makes a false representation of a material fact in the application for copyright registration provided for by section 409, or in any written statement filed in connection with the application, shall be fined not more than $2,500.

☆ U. S. GOVERNMENT PRINTING OFFICE : 1977 O - 248-641

# HOW TO FILL OUT FORM TX

Specific Instructions for Spaces 1-4

- The line-by-line instructions on this page are keyed to the spaces on the first page of Form TX, printed opposite.
- Please read through these instructions before you start filling out your application, and refer to the specific instructions for each space as you go along.

## SPACE 1: TITLE

• *Title of this Work:* Every work submitted for copyright registration must be given a title that is capable of identifying that particular work. If the copies or phonorecords of the work bear a title (or an identifying phrase that could serve as a title), transcribe its wording completely and exactly on the application. Remember that indexing of the registration and future identification of the work will depend on the information you give here.

• *Periodical or Serial Issue:* Periodicals and other serials are publications issued at intervals under a general title, such as newspapers, magazines, journals, newsletters, and annuals. If the work being registered is an entire issue of a periodical or serial, give the over-all title of the periodical or serial in the space headed "Title of this Work," and add the specific information about the issue in the spaces provided. If the work being registered is a contribution to a periodical or serial issue, follow the instructions for "Publication as a Contribution."

• *Previous or Alternative Titles:* Complete this space if there are any additional titles for the work under which someone searching for the registration might be likely to look, or under which a document pertaining to the work might be recorded.

• *Publication as a Contribution:* If the work being registered has been published as a contribution to a periodical, serial, or collection, give the title of the contribution in the space headed "Title of this Work." Then, in the line headed "Publication as a Contribution," give information about the larger work in which the contribution appeared.

## SPACE 2: AUTHORS

• *General Instructions:* First decide, after reading these instructions, who are the "authors" of this work for copyright purposes. Then, unless the work is a "collective work" (see below), give the requested information about every "author" who contributed any appreciable amount of copyrightable matter to this version of the work. If you need further space, use the attached Continuation Sheet and, if necessary, request additional Continuation Sheets (Form TX/Con).

• *Who is the "Author"?* Unless the work was "made for hire," the individual who actually created the work is its "author." In the case of a work made for you have checked "Yes" to indicate that the work was "made for hire," give the full legal name of the employer (or other person for whom the work was prepared). You may also include the name of the employee (for example, "Elster Publishing Co. employer for hire of John Ferguson"). If the work is "anonymous" you may: (1) leave the line blank, or (2) state "Anonymous" in the line, or (3) reveal the author's identity. If the work is "pseudonymous" you may (1) leave the line blank, or (2) give the pseudonym and identify it as such (for example: "Huntley Haverstock, pseudonym"), or (3) reveal the author's name, making clear which is the real name and which is the pseudonym (for example, "Judith Barton, whose pseudonym is Madeleine Elster")

hire, the statute provides that "the employer or other person for whom the work was prepared is considered the author."

• **What is a "Work Made for Hire"?** A "work made for hire" is defined as: (1) "a work prepared by an employee within the scope of his or her employment"; or (2) "a work specially ordered or commissioned" for certain uses specified in the statute, but only if there is a written agreement to consider it a "work made for hire."

• **Collective Work:** In the case of a collective work, such as a periodical issue, anthology, collection of essays, or encyclopedia, it is sufficient to give information about the author of the collective work as a whole.

• **Author's Identity Not Revealed:** If an author's contribution is "anonymous" or "pseudonymous," it is not necessary to give the name and dates for that author. However, the citizenship and domicile of the author **must** be given in all cases, and information about the nature of that author's contribution to the work should be included if possible.

• **Name of Author:** The fullest form of the author's name should be given. If

## SPACE 3: CREATION AND PUBLICATION

• **General Instructions:** Do not confuse "creation" with "publication." Every application for copyright registration must state "the year in which creation of the work was completed." Give the date and nation of first publication only if the work has been published.

• **Creation:** Under the statute, a work is "created" when it is fixed in a copy or phonorecord for the first time. Where a work has been prepared over a period of time, the part of the work existing in fixed form on a particular date constitutes the created work on that date. The date you give here should be the year in which the author completed the particular version for which registration

## SPACE 4: CLAIMANT(S)

• **Name(s) and Address(es) of Copyright Claimant(s):** Give the name(s) address(es) of the copyright claimant(s) in this work. The statute provides that copyright in a work belongs initially to the author of the work (including, in the case of a work made for hire, the employer or other person for whom the work was prepared). The copyright claimant is either the author of the work or a person or organization that has obtained ownership of the copyright initially belonging to the author.

• **Dates of Birth and Death:** If the author is dead, the statute requires that the year of death be included in the application unless the work is anonymous or pseudonymous. The author's birth date is optional, but is useful as a form of identification. Leave this space blank if the author's contribution was a "work made for hire."

• **"Anonymous" or "Pseudonymous" Work:** An author's contribution to a work is "anonymous" if that author is not identified on the copies or phonorecords of the work. An author's contribution to a work is "pseudonymous" if that author is identified on the copies or phonorecords under a fictitious name.

• **Author's Nationality or Domicile:** Give the country of which the author is a citizen, or the country in which the author is domiciled. The statute requires that either nationality or domicile be given in all cases.

• **Nature of Authorship:** After the words "Author of" give a brief general statement of the nature of this particular author's contribution to the work. Examples: "Entire text"; "Co-author of entire text"; "Chapters 11-14"; "Editorial revisions"; "Compilation and English translation"; "Illustrations."

is now being sought, even if other versions exist or if further changes or additions are planned.

• **Publication:** The statute defines "publication" as "the distribution of copies or phonorecords of a work to the public by sale or other transfer of ownership, or by rental, lease, or lending"; a work is also "published" if there has been an "offering to distribute copies or phonorecords to a group of persons for purposes of further distribution, public performance, or public display." Give the full date (month, day, year) when, and the country where, publication first occurred. If first publication took place simultaneously in the United States and other countries, it is sufficient to state "U.S.A."

• **Transfer:** The statute provides that, if the copyright claimant is not the author, the application for registration must contain "a brief statement of how the claimant obtained ownership of the copyright." If any copyright claimant named in space 4 is not an author named in space 2, give a brief, general statement summarizing the means by which that claimant obtained ownership of the copyright.

## PRIVACY ACT ADVISORY STATEMENT
**Required by the Privacy Act of 1974 (Public Law 93-579)**

AUTHORITY FOR REQUESTING THIS INFORMATION:
• Title 17, U.S.C. Secs. 409 and 410

FURNISHING THE REQUESTED INFORMATION IS:
• Voluntary

BUT IF THE INFORMATION IS NOT FURNISHED:
• It may be necessary to delay or refuse registration
• You may not be entitled to certain relief, remedies, and benefits provided in chapters 4 and 5 of title 17, U.S.C.

PRINCIPAL USES OF REQUESTED INFORMATION:
• Establishment and maintenance of a public record
• Examination of the application for compliance with legal requirements

OTHER ROUTINE USES:
• Public inspection and copying
• Preparation of public indexes

• Preparation of public catalogs of copyright registrations
• Preparation of search reports upon request

NOTE:
• No other advisory statement will be given you in connection with this application
• Please retain this statement and refer to it if we communicate with you regarding this application

# INSTRUCTIONS FOR FILLING OUT SPACES 5-11 OF FORM TX

## SPACE 5: PREVIOUS REGISTRATION

• **General Instructions:** The questions in space 5 are intended to find out whether an earlier registration has been made for this work and, if so, whether there is any basis for a new registration. As a general rule, only one basic copyright registration can be made for the same version of a particular work.

• **Same Version:** If this version is substantially the same as the work covered by a previous registration, a second registration is not generally possible unless: (1) the work has been registered in unpublished form and a second registration is now being sought to cover the first published edition, or (2) someone other than the author is identified as copyright claimant in the earlier registration, and the author is now seeking registration in his or her own name. If either

of these two exceptions apply, check the appropriate box and give the earlier registration number and date. Otherwise, do not submit Form TX; instead, write the Copyright Office for information about supplementary registration or recordation of transfers of copyright ownership.

• **Changed Version:** If the work has been changed, and you are now seeking registration to cover the additions or revisions, check the third box in space 5, give the earlier registration number and date, and complete both parts of space 6.

• **Previous Registration Number and Date:** If more than one previous registration has been made for the work, give the number and date of the latest registration.

## SPACE 6: COMPILATION OR DERIVATIVE WORK

• **General Instructions:** Complete both parts of space 6 if this work is a "compilation," or "derivative work," or both, and if it incorporates one or more earlier works that have already been published or registered for copyright, or that have fallen into the public domain. A "compilation" is defined as "a work formed by the collection and assembling of preexisting materials or of data that are selected, coordinated, or arranged in such a way that the resulting work as a whole constitutes an original work of authorship." A "derivative work" is "a work based on one or more preexisting works." Examples of derivative works include translations, fictionalizations, arrangements, abridgments, condensations, or "any other form in which a work may be recast, transformed, or adapted." Derivative works also include works "consisting of editorial revisions, annotations, elaborations, or other modifications" if these changes, as a whole, represent an original work of authorship.

• **Preexisting Material:** If the work is a compilation, give a brief, general statement describing the nature of the material that has been compiled. Example: "Compilation of all published 1917 speeches of Woodrow Wilson." In the case of a derivative work, identify the preexisting work that has been recast, transformed, or adapted. Example: "Russian version of Goncharov's 'Oblomov'."

• **Material Added to this Work:** The statute requires a "brief, general statement of the additional material covered by the copyright claim being registered." This statement should describe all of the material in this particular version of the work that: (1) represents an original work of authorship; and (2) has not fallen into the public domain; and (3) has not been previously published; and (4) has not been previously registered for copyright in unpublished form. Examples: "Foreword, selection, arrangement, editing, critical annotations"; "Revisions throughout; chapters 11-17 entirely new".

## SPACE 7: MANUFACTURING PROVISIONS

• **General Instructions:** The copyright statute currently provides, as a general rule, and with a number of exceptions, that the copies of a published work "consisting preponderantly of nondramatic literary material that is in the English language" be manufactured in the United States or Canada in order to be lawfully imported and publicly distributed in the United States. At the present time, applications for copyright registration covering published works that consist mainly of nondramatic text matter in English **must**, in most cases, identify those who performed certain processes in manufacturing the copies, together with the places where those processes were performed. *Please note:* The information must be given even if the copies were manufactured outside the United States or Canada; registration will be made regardless of the places of manufacture identified in space 7. In general, the processes covered

by this provision are: (1) typesetting and plate-making (where a typographic process preceded the actual printing); (2) the making of plates by a lithographic or photoengraving process (where this was a final or intermediate step before printing); and (3) the final printing and binding processes (in all cases). Leave space 7 blank if your work is unpublished or is not in English.

• *Import Statement:* As an exception to the manufacturing provisions, the statute prescribes that, where manufacture has taken place outside the United States or Canada, a maximum of 2000 copies of the foreign edition can be imported into the United States without affecting the copyright owner's rights. For this purpose, the Copyright Office will issue an import statement upon request and payment of a fee of $3 at the time of registration or at any later time. For further information about import statements, ask for circular R62.

## SPACE 8: REPRODUCTION FOR USE OF BLIND OR PHYSICALLY-HANDICAPPED PERSONS

• *General Instructions:* One of the major programs of the Library of Congress is to provide Braille editions and special recordings of works for the exclusive use of the blind and physically handicapped. In an effort to simplify and speed up the copyright licensing procedures that are a necessary part of this program, section 710 of the copyright statute provides for the establishment of a voluntary licensing system to be tied in with copyright registration. Under this system, the owner of copyright in a nondramatic literary work has the option, at the time of registration on Form TX, to grant to the Library of Congress a license to reproduce and distribute Braille editions and "talking books" or "talking magazines" of the work being registered. The Copyright Office regulations

provide that, under the license, the reproduction and distribution must be solely for the use of persons who are certified by competent authority as unable to read normal printed material as a result of physical limitations. The license is nonexclusive, and may be terminated upon 90 days notice. For further information, write for Circular R63.

• *How to Grant the License:* The license is entirely voluntary. If you wish to grant it, check one of the three boxes in space 8. Your check in one of these boxes, together with your signature in space 10, will mean that the Library of Congress can proceed to reproduce and distribute under the license without further paperwork.

## SPACES 9, 10, 11: FEE, CORRESPONDENCE, CERTIFICATION, RETURN ADDRESS

• *Deposit Account and Mailing Instructions (Space 9):* If you maintain a Deposit Account in the Copyright Office, identify it in space 9. Otherwise you will need to send the registration fee of $10 with your application. The space headed "Correspondence" should contain the name and address of the person to be consulted if correspondence about this application becomes necessary.

• *Certification (Space 10):* The application is not acceptable unless it bears the handwritten signature of the author or other copyright claimant, or of the owner of exclusive right(s), or of the duly authorized agent of such author, claimant, or owner.

• *Address for Return of Certificate (Space 11):* The address box must be completed legibly, since the certificate will be returned in a window envelope.

# FORM PA

UNITED STATES COPYRIGHT OFFICE
LIBRARY OF CONGRESS
WASHINGTON, D.C. 20559

# APPLICATION
# FOR
# COPYRIGHT
# REGISTRATION

*for a*
*Work of the Performing Arts*

## HOW TO APPLY FOR COPYRIGHT REGISTRATION:

- *First:* Read the information on this page to make sure Form PA is the correct application for your work.

- *Second:* Open out the form by pulling this page to the left. Read through the detailed instructions before starting to complete the form.

- *Third:* Complete spaces 1-4 of the application, then turn the entire form over and, after reading the instructions for spaces 5-9, complete the rest of your application. Use typewriter or print in dark ink. Be sure to sign the form at space 8.

- *Fourth:* Detach your completed application from these instructions and send it with the necessary deposit of the work (see below) to: Register of Copyrights, Library of Congress, Washington, D.C. 20559. Unless you have a Deposit

Account in the Copyright Office, your application and deposit must be accompanied by a check or money order for $10, payable to: *Register of Copyrights.*

**WHEN TO USE FORM PA:** Form PA is the appropriate application to use for copyright registration covering works of the performing arts. Both published and unpublished works can be registered on Form PA.

**WHAT IS A "WORK OF THE PERFORMING ARTS"?** This category includes works prepared for the purpose of being "performed" directly before an audience or indirectly "by means of any device or process." Examples of works of the performing arts are: (1) musical works, including any accompanying words; (2) dramatic works, including any accompanying music; (3) pantomimes and choreographic works; and (4) motion pictures and other audiovisual works. **Note:** This category does not include sound recordings, which should be registered on Form SR. For more information about copyright in sound recordings, see the reverse side of this sheet.

**DEPOSIT TO ACCOMPANY APPLICATION:** An application for copyright registration must be accompanied by a deposit representing the entire work for which registration is to be made. The following are the general deposit requirements as set forth in the statute:

*Unpublished work:* Deposit one complete copy or phonorecord.

*Published work:* Deposit two complete copies or phonorecords of the best edition.

*Work first published outside the United States:* Deposit one complete copy or phonorecord of the first foreign edition.

*Contribution to a collective work:* Deposit one complete copy or phonorecord of the best edition of the collective work.

These general deposit requirements may vary in particular situations. For further information about the specific deposit requirements for particular types of works of the performing arts, see the reverse side of this sheet. For general information about copyright deposit, write for Circular R7.

**THE COPYRIGHT NOTICE:** For published works, the law provides that a copyright notice in a specified form "shall be placed on all publicly distributed copies from which the work can be visually perceived." Use of the copyright notice is the responsibility of the copyright owner and does not require advance permission from the Copyright Office. The required form of the notice for copies generally consists of three elements: (1) the symbol "©", or the word "Copyright", or the abbreviation "Copr."; (2) the year of first publication; and (3) the name of the owner of copyright. For example: "© 1978 Alexander Hollenius". The notice is to be affixed to the copies "in such manner and location as to give reasonable notice of the claim of copyright." Unlike the law in effect before 1978, the new copyright statute provides procedures for correcting errors in the copyright notice, and even for curing the omission of the notice. However, a failure to comply with the notice requirements may still result in the loss of some copyright protection and, unless corrected within five years, in the complete loss of copyright. For further information about the copyright notice, see the reverse side of this sheet. For additional information concerning the copyright notice and the procedures for correcting errors or omissions, write for Circular R3.

**DURATION OF COPYRIGHT:** For works that were created after the effective date of the new statute (January 1, 1978), the basic copyright term will be the life of the author and fifty years after the author's death. For works made for hire, and for certain anonymous and pseudonymous works, the duration of copyright will be 75 years from publication or 100 years from creation, whichever is shorter. These same terms of copyright will generally apply to works that had been created before 1978 but had not been published or copyrighted before that date. For further information about the duration of copyright, including the terms of copyrights already in existence before 1978, write for Circular R15a.

# FORM PA

UNITED STATES COPYRIGHT OFFICE

REGISTRATION NUMBER

PA      PAU

EFFECTIVE DATE OF REGISTRATION

. . . . . . . . . .   . . . . . . . . .   . . . . . . . . . . .
Month      Day      Year

**DO NOT WRITE ABOVE THIS LINE. IF YOU NEED MORE SPACE, USE CONTINUATION SHEET (FORM PA/CON)**

**(1)** **Title**

**TITLE OF THIS WORK:**

**NATURE OF THIS WORK:**
(See instructions)

**PREVIOUS OR ALTERNATIVE TITLES:**

**(2)** **Author(s)**

**IMPORTANT:** Under the law, the "author" of a "work made for hire" is generally the employer, not the employee (see instructions). If any part of this work was "made for hire" check "Yes" in the space provided, give the employer (or other person for whom the work was prepared) as "Author" of that part, and leave the space for dates blank.

**NAME OF AUTHOR:**

**DATES OF BIRTH AND DEATH:**

Born . . . . . . . . Died . . . . . . . .
(Year)      (Year)

1

Was this author's contribution to the work a "work made for hire"?   Yes . . . . . .   No . . . . . .

**AUTHOR'S NATIONALITY OR DOMICILE:**

Citizen of . . . . . . . . . . . . . . . } or { Domiciled in . . . . . . . . . . . . . . . .
(Name of Country)            (Name of Country)

**AUTHOR OF:** (Briefly describe nature of this author's contribution)

**WAS THIS AUTHOR'S CONTRIBUTION TO THE WORK:**

Anonymous?   Yes . . . . . .   No . . . . . .
Pseudonymous?   Yes . . . . . .   No . . . . . .

If the answer to either of these questions is "Yes," see detailed instructions attached.

| **NAME OF AUTHOR:** | **DATES OF BIRTH AND DEATH:** |
|---|---|
| | Born ........ Died ........ |
| | (Year) (Year) |

**2**

Was this author's contribution to the work a "work made for hire"? Yes ....... No ......

**AUTHOR'S NATIONALITY OR DOMICILE:**

Citizen of ............ } or { Domiciled in ............
(Name of Country) (Name of Country)

**AUTHOR OF:** (Briefly describe nature of this author's contribution)

**WAS THIS AUTHOR'S CONTRIBUTION TO THE WORK:**

Anonymous? ....... Yes ....... No ......
Pseudonymous? Yes ....... No ......

If the answer to either of these questions is "Yes," see detailed instructions attached

---

| **NAME OF AUTHOR:** | **DATES OF BIRTH AND DEATH:** |
|---|---|
| | Born ........ Died ........ |
| | (Year) (Year) |

**3**

Was this author's contribution to the work a "work made for hire"? Yes ....... No ......

**AUTHOR'S NATIONALITY OR DOMICILE:**

Citizen of ............ } or { Domiciled in ............
(Name of Country) (Name of Country)

**AUTHOR OF:** (Briefly describe nature of this author's contribution)

**WAS THIS AUTHOR'S CONTRIBUTION TO THE WORK:**

Anonymous? ....... Yes ....... No ......
Pseudonymous? Yes ....... No ......

If the answer to either of these questions is "Yes," see detailed instructions attached.

---

**(3)**
**Creation and Publication**

**YEAR IN WHICH CREATION OF THIS WORK WAS COMPLETED:**

Year ............

(This information must be given in all cases.)

**DATE AND NATION OF FIRST PUBLICATION:**

Date ............ ............ ............
(Month) (Day) (Year)

Nation ............
(Name of Country)

(Complete this block ONLY if this work has been published)

---

**(4)**
**Claimant(s)**

**NAME(S) AND ADDRESS(ES) OF COPYRIGHT CLAIMANT(S):**

**TRANSFER:** (If the copyright claimant(s) named here in space 4 are different from the author(s) named in space 2, give a brief statement of how the claimant(s) obtained ownership of the copyright.)

---

**DO NOT WRITE HERE**

Page 1 of ....... pages

---

- Complete all applicable spaces (numbers 5-9) on the reverse side of this page.
- Follow detailed instructions attached.
- Sign the form at line 8.

| | EXAMINED BY: . . . . . . . . . . | APPLICATION RECEIVED: |
| | CHECKED BY: . . . . . . . . . . | |
| FOR COPYRIGHT OFFICE USE ONLY | CORRESPONDENCE: ☐ Yes | DEPOSIT RECEIVED: |
| | DEPOSIT ACCOUNT FUNDS USED: ☐ | REMITTANCE NUMBER AND DATE: |

**DO NOT WRITE ABOVE THIS LINE. IF YOU NEED ADDITIONAL SPACE, USE CONTINUATION SHEET (FORM PA/CON)**

**(5) Previous Registration**

**PREVIOUS REGISTRATION:**

• Has registration for this work, or for an earlier version of this work, already been made in the Copyright Office? Yes . . . . . . . . . No . . . . . . . . .

• If your answer is "Yes," why is another registration being sought? (Check appropriate box)

☐ This is the first published edition of a work previously registered in unpublished form.

☐ This is the first application submitted by this author as copyright claimant.

☐ This is a changed version of the work, as shown by line 6 of the application.

• If your answer is "Yes," give: Previous Registration Number . . . . . . . . . . . . . . . . . . . . . . Year of Registration . . . . . . . . . . . . . . . . . . . .

**(6) Compilation or Derivative Work**

**COMPILATION OR DERIVATIVE WORK:** (See instructions)

PREEXISTING MATERIAL: (Identify any preexisting work or works that the work is based on or incorporates.)

. . . . . . . . . . . . . . . . . . . . . . . . . . . . . . . . . . . . . . . . . . . . . . . . . . . . . . . . . . . . . . . . . . . . . .

. . . . . . . . . . . . . . . . . . . . . . . . . . . . . . . . . . . . . . . . . . . . . . . . . . . . . . . . . . . . . . . . . . . . . .

. . . . . . . . . . . . . . . . . . . . . . . . . . . . . . . . . . . . . . . . . . . . . . . . . . . . . . . . . . . . . . . . . . . . . .

MATERIAL ADDED TO THIS WORK: (Give a brief, general statement of the material that has been added to this work and in which copyright is claimed.)

**DEPOSIT ACCOUNT:** (If the registration fee is to be charged to a Deposit Account established in the Copyright Office, give name and number of Account.)

Name: .......................................................

Account Number: .............................................

**CORRESPONDENCE:** (Give name and address to which correspondence about this application should be sent.)

Name: .......................................................

Address: ....................................................

.......................... (Apt.)

........................ (City) .............. (State) .......... (ZIP)

(7) Fee and Correspondence

**CERTIFICATION:** ✱ I, the undersigned, hereby certify that I am the: (Check one)

☐ author ☐ other copyright claimant ☐ owner of exclusive right(s) ☐ authorized agent of: .................... (Name of author or other copyright claimant, or owner of exclusive right(s))

of the work identified in this application and that the statements made by me in this application are correct to the best of my knowledge.

Handwritten signature: (X) .................................

Date ............................

Typed or printed name. ......................................

(8) Certification (Application must be signed)

**MAIL CERTIFICATE TO**

(Certificate will be mailed in window envelope)

................................................ (Name)

................................................ (Number, Street and Apartment Number)

................................................ (City) ........................ (State) ........ (ZIP code)

(9) Address For Return of Certificate

Nov. 1977 - 1,000,000

# HOW TO FILL OUT FORM PA

Specific Instructions for Spaces 1-4

- The line-by-line instructions on this page are keyed to the spaces on the first page of Form PA, printed opposite.
- Please read through these instructions before you start filling out your application, and refer to the specific instructions for each space as you go along.

## SPACE 1: TITLE

- **Title of this Work:** Every work submitted for copyright registration must be given a title that is capable of identifying that particular work. If the copies or phonorecords of the work bear a title (or an identifying phrase that could serve as a title), transcribe its wording completely and exactly on the application. Remember that indexing of the registration and future identification of the work will depend on the information you give here.

If the work you are registering is an entire "collective work" (such as a collection of plays or songs), give the over-all title of the collection. If you are registering one or more individual contributions to a collective work, give the title of

each contribution, followed by the title of the collection. Example: "'A Song for Elinda' in *Old and New Ballads for Old and New People.*"

- **Nature of this Work:** Briefly describe the general nature or character of the work being registered for copyright. Examples: "Music"; "Song Lyrics"; "Words and Music"; "Drama"; "Musical Play"; "Choreography"; "Pantomime"; "Motion Picture"; "Audiovisual Work".
- **Previous or Alternative Titles:** Complete this space if there are any additional titles for the work under which someone searching for the registration might be likely to look, or under which a document pertaining to the work might be recorded.

## SPACE 2: AUTHORS

- **General Instructions:** First decide, after reading these instructions, who are the "authors" of this work for copyright purposes. Then, unless the work is a "collective work" (see below), give the requested information about every "author" who contributed any appreciable amount of copyrightable matter to this version of the work. If you need further space, use the attached Continuation Sheet and, if necessary, request additional Continuation Sheets (Form PA/Con).
- **Who is the "Author"?** Unless the work was "made for hire," the individual who actually created the work is its "author." In the case of a work made for

full legal name of the employer (or other person for whom the work was prepared). You may also include the name of the employee (for example: "Music Makers Publishing Co., employer for hire of Lila Crane"). If the work is "anonymous" you may: (1) leave the line blank, or (2) state "Anonymous" in the line, or (3) reveal the author's identity. If the work is "pseudonymous" you may: (1) leave the line blank, or (2) give the pseudonym and identify it as such (for example: "Huntley Haverstock, pseudonym"), or (3) reveal the author's name, making clear which is the real name and which is the pseudonym (for example, "Judith Barton, whose pseudonym is Madeleine Elster").

work was prepared is considered the author.

• **What is a "Work Made for Hire"?** A "work made for hire" is defined as: (1) "a work prepared by an employee within the scope of his or her employment"; or (2) "a work specially ordered or commissioned" for certain uses specified in the statute, but only if there is a written agreement to consider it a "work made for hire."

• **Collective Work:** In the case of a collective work, such as a song book or a collection of plays, it is sufficient to give information about the author of the collective work as a whole.

• **Author's Identity Not Revealed:** If an author's contribution is "anonymous" or "pseudonymous," it is not necessary to give the name and dates for that author. However, the citizenship and domicile of the author **must** be given in all cases, and information about the nature of that author's contribution to the work should be included if possible.

• **Name of Author:** The fullest form of the author's name should be given. If you have checked "Yes" to indicate that the work was "made for hire," give the year of death be included in the application unless the work is anonymous or pseudonymous. The author's birth date is optional, but is useful as a form of identification. Leave this space blank if the author's contribution was a "work made for hire."

• **"Anonymous" or "Pseudonymous" Work:** An author's contribution to a work is "anonymous" if that author is not identified on the copies or phonorecords of the work. An author's contribution to a work is "pseudonymous" if that author is identified on the copies or phonorecords under a fictitious name.

• **Author's Nationality or Domicile:** Give the country of which the author is a citizen, or the country in which the author is domiciled. The statute requires that either nationality or domicile be given in all cases.

• **Nature of Authorship:** After the words "Author of" give a brief general statement of the nature of this particular author's contribution to the work. Examples: "Words"; "Co-Author of Music"; "Words and Music"; "Arrangement"; "Co-Author of Book and Lyrics"; "Dramatization"; "Entire Work"; "Compilation and English Translation"; "Editorial Revisions".

## SPACE 3: CREATION AND PUBLICATION

• **General Instructions:** Do not confuse "creation" with "publication." Every application for copyright registration must state "the year in which creation of the work was completed." Give the date and nation of first publication only if the work has been published.

• **Creation:** Under the statute, a work is "created" when it is fixed in a copy or phonorecord for the first time. Where a work has been prepared over a period of time, the part of the work existing in fixed form on a particular date constitutes the created work on that date. The date you give here should be the year in which the author completed the particular version for which registration is now being sought, even if other versions exist or if further changes or additions are planned.

• **Publication:** The statute defines "publication" as "the distribution of copies or phonorecords of a work to the public by sale or other transfer of ownership, or by rental, lease, or lending"; a work is also "published" if there has been an "offering to distribute copies or phonorecords to a group of persons for purposes of further distribution, public performance, or public display." Give the full date (month, day, year) when, and the country where, publication first occurred. If first publication took place simultaneously in the United States and other countries, it is sufficient to state "U.S.A."

## SPACE 4: CLAIMANT(S)

• **Name(s) and Address(es) of Copyright Claimant(s):** Give the name(s) and address(es) of the copyright claimant(s) in this work. The statute provides that copyright in a work belongs initially to the author of the work (including, in the case of a work made for hire, the employer or other person for whom the work was prepared). The copyright claimant is either the author of the work or a person or organization that has obtained ownership of the copyright initially belonging to the author.

• **Transfer:** The statute provides that, if the copyright claimant is not the author, the application for registration must contain "a brief statement of how the claimant obtained ownership of the copyright." If any copyright claimant named in space 4 is not an author named in space 2, give a brief general statement summarizing the means by which that claimant obtained ownership of the copyright.

## PRIVACY ACT ADVISORY STATEMENT
### Required by the Privacy Act of 1974 (Public Law 93-579)

AUTHORITY FOR REQUESTING THIS INFORMATION:
- Title 17, U.S.C., Secs. 409 and 410

FURNISHING THE REQUESTED INFORMATION IS
- Voluntary

BUT IF THE INFORMATION IS NOT FURNISHED:
- It may be necessary to delay or refuse registration
- You may not be entitled to certain relief, remedies, and benefits provided in chapters 4 and 5 of title 17, U.S.C.

PRINCIPAL USES OF REQUESTED INFORMATION:
- Establishment and maintenance of a public record
- Examination of the application for compliance with legal requirements

OTHER ROUTINE USES:
- Public inspection and copying
- Preparation of public indexes
- Preparation of public catalogs of copyright registrations
- Preparation of search reports upon request

NOTE:
- No other advisory statement will be given you in connection with this application
- Please retain this statement and refer to it if we communicate with you regarding this application

# INSTRUCTIONS FOR SPACES 5-9

## SPACE 5: PREVIOUS REGISTRATION

• **General Instructions:** The questions in space 5 are intended to find out whether an earlier registration has been made for this work and, if so, whether there is any basis for a new registration. As a general rule, only one basic copyright registration can be made for the same version of a particular work.

• **Same Version:** If this version is substantially the same as the work covered by a previous registration, a second registration is not generally possible unless: (1) the work has been registered in unpublished form and a second registration is now being sought to cover the first published edition, or (2) someone other than the author is identified as copyright claimant in the earlier registration, and the author is now seeking registration in his or her own name. If either of these two exceptions apply, check the appropriate box and give the earlier registration number and date. Otherwise, do not submit Form PA; instead, write the Copyright Office for information about supplementary registration or recordation of transfers of copyright ownership.

• **Changed Version:** If the work has been changed, and you are now seeking registration to cover the additions or revisions, check the third box in space 5, give the earlier registration number and date, and complete both parts of space 6.

• **Previous Registration Number and Date:** If more than one previous registration has been made for the work, give the number and date of the latest registration.

## SPACE 6: COMPILATION OR DERIVATIVE WORK

• **General Instructions:** Complete both parts of space 6 if this work is a

# MORE INFORMATION

**A NOTE ON TERMINOLOGY:** The following are the meanings given to some of the terms used in the copyright statute:

• **"Works":** "Works" are the basic subject matter of copyright; they are what authors create and copyright protects. The statute draws a sharp distinction between the "work" and "any material object in which the work is embodied."

• **"Copies" and "Phonorecords":** These are the two types of material objects in which "works" are embodied. In general, **"copies"** are objects from which a work can be read or visually perceived, directly or with the aid of a machine or device, such as manuscripts, books, sheet music, film, and videotape. **"Phonorecords"** are objects embodying fixations of sounds, such as audio tapes and phonograph disks. For example, a song (the "work") can be reproduced in sheet music ("copies") or phonograph disks ("phonorecords"), or both.

• **"Sound Recordings":** These are "works," not "copies" or "phonorecords." With one exception, "sound recordings" are "works that result from the fixation of a series of musical, spoken, or other sounds." (The exception is for the audio portions of audiovisual works, including motion picture soundtracks; these are considered an integral part of the audiovisual work as a whole.) "Sound recordings" are registered on Form SR.

**Example:** When a record company issues a new release, the release will typically involve two distinct "works": the "musical work" that has been recorded, and the "sound recording" as a separate work in itself. The material objects that the record company sends out are "phonorecords": physical reproductions of both the "musical work" and the "sound recording."

## FOR A MUSICAL OR DRAMATIC WORK, SHOULD YOU DEPOSIT COPIES OR PHONORECORDS WITH YOUR FORM PA?

• **For registration in unpublished form:**

(1) If the work exists only in one form or the other (copies or phonorecords, but not both), deposit the work in its existing form.

(2) If the work exists in both copies and phonorecords, deposit the form that best represents the musical or dramatic work in which copyright is being claimed.

• **For registration in published form:**

(1) If the work has been published in the form of copies but not phonorecords, deposit two copies of the best edition. If the work has been published in the form of phonorecords only, deposit two phonorecords of the best edition.

(2) If the work has been published in both forms, deposit two copies (**not phonorecords**) of the best edition.

(3) If the work has been first published outside the United States, deposit one copy or phonorecord as first published.

**SHOULD YOU FILE FORM PA OR FORM SR?** If the musical or dramatic work has been recorded, and both that "work," and the sound recording as a separate "work," are eligible for registration, the application form you should file depends on the following:

• **File only Form PA if:** You are seeking to register only the musical or dramatic work, not the sound recording.

• **File only Form SR if:** The copyright claimant for both the musical or dramatic work and the sound recording is the same, and you are seeking a single registration to cover both of these "works."

• **Separate applications on Forms PA and SR should be filed if:**

(1) The copyright claimant for the musical or dramatic work is different from the copyright claimant for the sound recording; or

(2) You prefer to have separate registrations for the musical or dramatic work and the sound recording.

**FORM OF COPYRIGHT NOTICE ON PHONORECORDS:**

**For musical or dramatic works:** The copyright notice for musical and dramatic works (for example: "© 1978 George Harvey Bone") is required to appear on "all publicly distributed copies from which the work can be visually perceived." There is no requirement that the notice for musical or dramatic works be placed on phonorecords reproducing them.

**For sound recordings:** The copyright statute provides that, whenever a sound recording is published, a special notice of copyright (for example: "℗1978 Miriam Haines") "shall be placed on all publicly distributed phonorecords of the sound recording." For further information about the requirements for copyright in sound recordings, write for Form SR and Circular R56.

---

earlier works that have already been published or registered for copyright, or that have fallen into the public domain. A "compilation" is defined as "a work formed by the collection and assembling of preexisting materials or of data that are selected, coordinated, or arranged in such a way that the resulting work as a whole constitutes an original work of authorship." A "derivative work" is "a work based on one or more preexisting works." Examples of derivative works include musical arrangements, dramatizations, translations, abridgments, condensations, motion picture versions, or "any other form in which a work may be recast, transformed, or adapted." Derivative works also include works "consisting of editorial revisions, annotations, elaborations, or other modifications" if these changes, as a whole, represent an original work of authorship.

• **Preexisting Material:** If the work is a compilation, give a brief, general statement describing the nature of the material that has been compiled. Example: "Compilation of 19th Century military songs." In the case of a derivative work, identify the preexisting work that has been recast, transformed, or adapted. Example: "French version of Hugo's 'Le Roi s'amuse.'"

• **Material Added to this Work:** The statute requires a "brief, general statement of the additional material covered by the copyright claim being registered." This statement should describe all of the material in this particular version of the work that: (1) represents an original work of authorship; and (2) has not fallen into the public domain; and (3) has not been previously published; and (4) has not been previously registered for copyright in unpublished form. Examples: "Arrangement for piano and orchestra"; "Dramatization for television"; "New film version"; "Revisions throughout: Act III completely new."

## SPACES 7, 8, 9: FEE, CORRESPONDENCE, CERTIFICATION, RETURN ADDRESS

• **Deposit Account and Mailing Instructions (Space 7):** If you maintain a Deposit Account in the Copyright Office, identify it in space 7. Otherwise you will need to send the registration fee of $10 with your application. The space headed "Correspondence" should contain the name and address of the person to be consulted if correspondence about this application becomes necessary.

• **Certification (Space 8):** The application is not acceptable unless it bears the handwritten signature of the author or other copyright claimant, or of the owner of exclusive right(s), or of the duly authorized agent of such author, claimant, or owner.

• **Address for Return of Certificate (Space 9):** The address box must be completed legibly, since the certificate will be returned in a window envelope.

# FORM VA

UNITED STATES COPYRIGHT OFFICE
LIBRARY OF CONGRESS
WASHINGTON, D.C. 20559

# APPLICATION
# FOR
# COPYRIGHT
# REGISTRATION

*for a*
*Work of the Visual Arts*

## HOW TO APPLY FOR COPYRIGHT REGISTRATION:

- **First:** Read the information on this page to make sure Form VA is the correct application for your work.

- **Second:** Open out the form by pulling this page to the left. Read through the detailed instructions before starting to complete the form.

- **Third:** Complete spaces 1-4 of the application, then turn the entire form over and, after reading the instructions for spaces 5-9, complete the rest of your application. Use typewriter or print in dark ink. Be sure to sign the form at space 8.

- **Fourth:** Detach your completed application from these instructions and send it with the necessary deposit of the work (see below) to: Register of Copyrights, Library of Congress, Washington, D.C. 20559. Unless you have a Deposit

companied by a check or money order for $10, payable to: *Register of Copyrights.*

**WHEN TO USE FORM VA:** Form VA is the appropriate form to use for copyright registration covering works of the visual arts. Both published and unpublished works can be registered on Form VA.

**WHAT IS A "WORK OF THE VISUAL ARTS"?** This category consists of "pictorial, graphic, or sculptural works," including two-dimensional and three-dimensional works of fine, graphic, and applied art, photographs, prints and art reproductions, maps, globes, charts, technical drawings, diagrams, and models.

**WHAT DOES COPYRIGHT PROTECT?** Copyright in a work of the visual arts protects those pictorial, graphic, or sculptural elements that, either alone or in combination, represent an "original work of authorship." The statute declares: "In no case does copyright protection for an original work of authorship extend to any idea, procedure, process, system, method of operation, concept, principle, or discovery, regardless of the form in which it is described, explained, illustrated, or embodied in such work."

**WORKS OF ARTISTIC CRAFTSMANSHIP AND DESIGNS:** "Works of artistic craftsmanship" are registrable on Form VA, but the statute makes clear that protection extends to "their form" and not to "their mechanical or utilitarian aspects." The "design of a useful article" is considered copyrightable "only if, and only to the extent that, such design incorporates pictorial, graphic, or sculptural features that can be identified separately from, and are capable of existing independently of, the utilitarian aspects of the article."

**LABELS AND ADVERTISEMENTS:** Works prepared for use in connection with the sale or advertisement of goods and services are registrable if they contain "original work of authorship." Use Form VA if the copyrightable material in the work you are registering is mainly pictorial or graphic; use Form TX if it consists mainly of text. NOTE: Words and short phrases such as names, titles, and slogans cannot be protected by copyright, and the same is true of standard symbols, emblems, and other commonly-used graphic designs that are in the public domain. When used commercially, material of that sort can sometimes be protected un-

der State laws of unfair competition or under the Federal trademark laws. For information about trademark registration, write to the Commissioner of Patents and Trademarks, Washington, D.C. 20231.

**DEPOSIT TO ACCOMPANY APPLICATION:** An application for copyright registration must be accompanied by a deposit representing the entire work for which registration is to be made. The following are the general deposit requirements for works of the visual arts, as set forth in the statute:

*Unpublished work:* Deposit one complete copy.

*Published work:* Deposit two complete copies of the best edition.

*Work first published outside the United States:* Deposit one complete copy of the first foreign edition.

*Contribution to a collective work:* Deposit one complete copy of the best edition of the collective work.

These general deposit requirements will vary in particular situations. In most cases, where the copies in which the work has been reproduced are three-dimensional, the Copyright Office Regulations provide for the deposit of identifying material (such as photographs or drawings) meeting certain requirements. For further information about the deposit requirements for works of the visual arts, see the reverse side of this sheet. For general information about copyright deposit, write to the Copyright Office.

**DURATION OF COPYRIGHT:** For works that were created after the effective date of the new statute (January 1, 1978), the basic copyright term will be the life of the author and fifty years after the author's death. For works made for hire, and for certain anonymous and pseudonymous works, the duration of copyright will be 75 years from publication or 100 years from creation, whichever is shorter. These same terms of copyright will generally apply to works that had been created before 1978 but had not been published or copyrighted before that date. For further information about the duration of copyright, including the terms of copyrights already in existence before 1978, write for Circular R15a.

# FORM VA
UNITED STATES COPYRIGHT OFFICE

REGISTRATION NUMBER

VA     VAU

EFFECTIVE DATE OF REGISTRATION

. . . . . . . . . . . . . . . . . . . . . . .
(Month)     (Day)     (Year)

---

**DO NOT WRITE ABOVE THIS LINE. IF YOU NEED MORE SPACE, USE CONTINUATION SHEET (FORM VA/CON)**

**(1) Title**

**TITLE OF THIS WORK:**     **NATURE OF THIS WORK:** (See instructions)

Previous or Alternative Titles:

**PUBLICATION AS A CONTRIBUTION:** (If this work was published as a contribution to a periodical, serial, or collection, give information about the collective work in which the contribution appeared.)

Title of Collective Work: . . . . . . . . . . . . . . . . . . . . . . . . . . . . . . . . . . . . . . . . . Vol. . . . . . No. . . . . . Date . . . . . . . . . . . . . . . Pages . . . . . . . . . .

**(2) Author(s)**

**IMPORTANT:** Under the law, the "author" of a "work made for hire" is generally the employer, not the employee (see instructions). If any part of this work was "made for hire" check "Yes" in the space provided, give the employer (or other person for whom the work was prepared) as "Author" of that part, and leave the space for dates blank.

**NAME OF AUTHOR:**     **DATES OF BIRTH AND DEATH:**

Born . . . . . . (Year)   Died . . . . . . (Year)

**1**

Was this author's contribution to the work a "work made for hire"?   Yes . . . . . . No . . . . . .

**AUTHOR'S NATIONALITY OR DOMICILE:**

Citizen of . . . . . . . . . . . . . . . } or { Domiciled in . . . . . . . . . . . . . . .
    (Name of Country)               (Name of Country)

**AUTHOR OF:** (Briefly describe nature of this author's contribution)

**WAS THIS AUTHOR'S CONTRIBUTION TO THE WORK:**

Anonymous?   Yes . . . . . . No . . . . . .
Pseudonymous?   Yes . . . . . . No . . . . . .

If the answer to either of these questions is "Yes," see detailed instructions attached.

**2**

**NAME OF AUTHOR:**

DATES OF BIRTH AND DEATH:
Born ........ Died ........
(Year)     (Year)

Was this author's contribution to the work a "work made for hire"? Yes ....... No .....

**AUTHOR'S NATIONALITY OR DOMICILE:**

Citizen of ................ } or { Domiciled in .............
(Name of Country)                    (Name of Country)

WAS THIS AUTHOR'S CONTRIBUTION TO THE WORK:
Anonymous?       Yes ...... No .....
Pseudonymous?   Yes ...... No .....

If the answer to either of these questions is "Yes," see detailed instructions attached.

**AUTHOR OF:** (Briefly describe nature of this author's contribution)

**3**

**NAME OF AUTHOR:**

DATES OF BIRTH AND DEATH:
Born ........ Died ........
(Year)     (Year)

Was this author's contribution to the work a "work made for hire"? Yes ....... No .....

**AUTHOR'S NATIONALITY OR DOMICILE:**

Citizen of ................ } or { Domiciled in .............
(Name of Country)                    (Name of Country)

WAS THIS AUTHOR'S CONTRIBUTION TO THE WORK:
Anonymous?       Yes ...... No .....
Pseudonymous?   Yes ...... No .....

If the answer to either of these questions is "Yes," see detailed instructions attached.

**AUTHOR OF:** (Briefly describe nature of this author's contribution)

---

**3**

**Creation and Publication**

**YEAR IN WHICH CREATION OF THIS WORK WAS COMPLETED:**

Year. ............
(This information must be given in all cases.)

**DATE AND NATION OF FIRST PUBLICATION:**

Date ............
(Month)          (Day)          (Year)

Nation ............
(Name of Country)
(Complete this block ONLY if this work has been published.)

---

**4**

**Claimant(s)**

**NAME(S) AND ADDRESS(ES) OF COPYRIGHT CLAIMANT(S):**

**TRANSFER:** (If the copyright claimant(s) named here in space 4 are different from the author(s) named in space 2, give a brief statement of how the claimant(s) obtained ownership of the copyright.)

---

DO NOT WRITE HERE
Page 1 of ........ pages

• Complete all applicable spaces (numbers 5-9) on the reverse side of this page
• Follow detailed instructions attached   • Sign the form at line 8

| | EXAMINED BY: .......... | APPLICATION RECEIVED: | |
| | CHECKED BY: .......... | | FOR COPYRIGHT OFFICE USE ONLY |
| | CORRESPONDENCE: ☐ Yes | DEPOSIT RECEIVED: | |
| | DEPOSIT ACCOUNT FUNDS USED: ☐ | REMITTANCE NUMBER AND DATE: | |

**DO NOT WRITE ABOVE THIS LINE. IF YOU NEED ADDITIONAL SPACE, USE CONTINUATION SHEET (FORM VA/CON)**

**PREVIOUS REGISTRATION:**

- Has registration for this work, or for an earlier version of this work, already been made in the Copyright Office? Yes. ........ No. ........

- If your answer is "Yes," why is another registration being sought? (Check appropriate box)
  ☐ This is the first published edition of a work previously registered in unpublished form.
  ☐ This is the first application submitted by this author as copyright claimant.
  ☐ This is a changed version of the work, as shown by line 6 of the application.

- If your answer is "Yes," give: Previous Registration Number. .......................... Year of Registration. ..........................

**⑤ Previous Registration**

**COMPILATION OR DERIVATIVE WORK:** (See instructions)

PREEXISTING MATERIAL: (Identify any preexisting work or works that this work is based on or incorporates.)
.............................................
.............................................
.............................................
.............................................

MATERIAL ADDED TO THIS WORK: (Give a brief, general statement of the material that has been added to this work and in which copyright is claimed.)

**⑥ Compilation or Derivative Work**

**DEPOSIT ACCOUNT:** (If the registration fee is to be charged to a Deposit Account established in the Copyright Office, give name and number of Account.)

Name: ...........................................................

Account Number: ...........................................................

**(7)**

**Fee and Correspondence**

**CORRESPONDENCE:** (Give name and address to which correspondence about this application should be sent.)

Name: ...........................................................

Address: ...........................................................

................ (City) ................ (State) ................ (ZIP)

**CERTIFICATION:** ✱ I, the undersigned, hereby certify that I am the: (Check one)

☐ author ☐ other copyright claimant ☐ owner of exclusive right(s) ☐ authorized agent of: ................ (Name of author or other copyright claimant, or owner of exclusive right(s))

of the work identified in this application and that the statements made by me in this application are correct to the best of my knowledge.

Handwritten signature: (X) ...........................................................

Typed or printed name: ................................ Date: ................

**(8)**

**Certification**

**(Application must be signed)**

**MAIL CERTIFICATE TO**

(Certificate will be mailed in window envelope)

................................................................
(Name)

................................................................
(Number, Street and Apartment Number)

................ (City) ................ (State) ................ (ZIP code)

**(9)**

**Address For Return of Certificate**

✱ 17 U.S.C. § 506(e): FALSE REPRESENTATION — Any person who knowingly makes a false representation of a material fact in the application for copyright registration provided for by section 409, or in any written statement filed in connection with the application, shall be fined not more than $2,500.

☆ U.S. GOVERNMENT PRINTING OFFICE: 1978—261-022/4

Jan. 1978—300,000

# HOW TO FILL OUT FORM VA

## Specific Instructions for Spaces 1-4

- The line-by-line instructions on this page are keyed to the spaces on the first page of Form VA, printed opposite.

- Please read through these instructions before you start filling out your application, and refer to the specific instructions for each space as you go along.

## SPACE 1: TITLE

- **Title of this Work:** Every work submitted for copyright registration must be given a title that is capable of identifying that particular work. If the copies of the work bear a title (or an identifying phrase that could serve as a title), transcribe its wording completely and exactly on the application; otherwise give the work a short descriptive title. Making it as explicit as possible. Remember that index-ing of the registration and future identification of the work will depend on the information you give here.

- **Previous or Alternative Titles:** Complete this line if there are any addi-tional titles for this work under which someone searching for the registration

## SPACE 2: AUTHORS

- **General Instructions:** First decide, after reading these instructions, who are the "authors" of this work for copyright purposes. Then, unless the work is a "collective work" (see below), give the requested information about every "author" who contributed any appreciable amount of copyrightable matter to this version of the work. If you need further space, use the attached Continua-tion Sheet and, if necessary, request additional Continuation Sheets (Form VA/CON).

- **Who is the "Author"?** Unless the work was "made for hire," the individual who actually created the work is its "author." In the case of works of the visual arts, "authors" include artists, cartographers, sculptors, painters, photographers,

might be likely to look, or under which a document pertaining to the work might be recorded.

- **Publication as a Contribution:** If the work being registered has been published as a contribution to a periodical, serial, or collection, give the title of the contribution in the space headed "Title of this Work." Then, in the line headed "Publication as a Contribution," give information about the larger work in which the contribution appeared.

- **Nature of this Work:** Briefly describe the nature or character of the pictor-ial, graphic, or sculptural work being registered for copyright. Examples: "Oil Painting"; "Charcoal Drawing"; "Etching"; "Sculpture"; "Map"; "Photograph"; "Scale Model"; "Lithographic Print"; "Jewelry Design"; "Fabric Design"

- **Name of Author:** The fullest form of the author's name should be given. If you have checked "Yes" to indicate that the work was "made for hire," give the full legal name of the employer (or other person for whom the work was pre-pared). You may also include the name of the employee (for example: "Fre-mont Enterprises, Inc. employer for hire of L.B. Jeffries"). If the work is "anon-ymous" you may: (1) leave the line blank, or (2) state "Anonymous" in the line, or (3) reveal the author's identity. If the work is "pseudonymous" you may (1) leave the line blank, or (2) give the pseudonym and identify it as such (for ex-ample: "Richard Heldar, pseudonym"), or (3) reveal the author's name, making clear which is the real name and which is the pseudonym (for example: "Henry Leek, whose pseudonym is Priam Farrel").

printmakers, and all others who create pictorial, graphic, or sculptural material. Where a work is made for hire, the statute provides that "the employer or other person for whom the work was prepared is considered the author."

• **What is a "Work Made for Hire"?** A "work made for hire" is defined as: (1) "a work prepared by an employee within the scope of his or her employment"; or (2) "a work specially ordered or commissioned" for certain uses specified in the statute, but only if there is a written agreement to consider it a "work made for hire."

• **Collective Work:** In the case of a collective work, such as a catalog of paintings or a collection of cartoons by various artists, it is sufficient to give information about the author of the collective work as a whole.

• **Author's Identity Not Revealed:** If an author's contribution is "anonymous" or "pseudonymous," it is not necessary to give the name and dates for that author. However, the citizenship or domicile of the author **must be given** in all cases, and information about the nature of that author's contribution to the work should be included.

• **Dates of Birth and Death:** If the author is dead, the statute requires that the year of death be included in the application unless the work is anonymous or pseudonymous. The author's birth date is optional, but is useful as a form of identification. Leave this space blank if the author's contribution was a "work made for hire."

• **"Anonymous" or "Pseudonymous" Work:** An author's contribution to a work is "anonymous" if that author is not identified on the copies of the work. An author's contribution to a work is "pseudonymous" if that author is identified on the copies under a fictitious name.

• **Author's Nationality or Domicile:** Give the country of which the author is a citizen, or the country in which the author is domiciled. The statute requires that either nationality or domicile be given in all cases.

• **Nature of Authorship:** After the words "Author of" give a brief general statement of the nature of this particular author's contribution to the work. Examples: "Painting"; "Photograph"; "Silk Screen Reproduction"; "Co author of Cartographic Material"; "Technical Drawing"; "Text and Artwork."

## SPACE 3: CREATION AND PUBLICATION

• **General Instructions:** Do not confuse "creation" with "publication." Every application for copyright registration must state "the year in which creation of the work was completed." Give the date and nation of first publication only if the work has been published.

• **Creation:** Under the statute, a work of the visual arts is "created" when it is fixed in a copy for the first time. A work is "fixed" in a copy when its embodiment "is sufficiently permanent or stable to permit it to be perceived, reproduced, or otherwise communicated for a period of more than transitory duration." Where a work has been prepared over a period of time, the part of the work existing in fixed form on a particular date constitutes the created work on that date. The date you give here should be the year in which the author completed the particular version for which registration is now being sought, even if other versions exist or if further changes or additions are planned.

• **Publication:** "Publication" is defined as "the distribution of copies or phonorecords of a work to the public by sale or other transfer of ownership, or by rental, lease, or lending"; a work is also "published" if there has been an "offering to distribute copies or phonorecords to a group of persons for purposes of further distribution, public performance, or public display." The statute makes clear that public display of a work "does not of itself constitute publication." Give the full date (month, day, year) when, and the country where, publication first occurred. If first publication took place simultaneously in the United States and other countries, it is sufficient to state "U.S.A."

## SPACE 4: CLAIMANT(S)

• **Name(s) and Address(es) of Copyright Claimant(s):** Give the name(s) and address(es) of the copyright claimant(s) in this work. The statute provides that copyright in a work belongs initially to the author of the work (including, in the case of a work made for hire, the employer or other person for whom the work was prepared). The copyright claimant is either the author of the work or a person or organization that has obtained ownership of the copyright initially belonging to the author.

• **Transfer:** The statute provides that, if the copyright claimant is not the author, the application for registration must contain "a brief statement of how the claimant obtained ownership of the copyright." If any copyright claimant named in space 4 is not an author named in space 2, give a brief, general statement summarizing the means by which that claimant obtained ownership of the copyright.

# INSTRUCTIONS FOR SPACES 5-9

## SPACE 5: PREVIOUS REGISTRATION

• **General Instructions:** The questions in space 5 are intended to find out whether an earlier registration has been made for this work and, if so, whether there is any basis for a new registration. As a general rule, only one basic copyright registration can be made for the same version of a particular work.

• **Same Version:** If this version is substantially the same as the work covered by a previous registration, a second registration is not generally possible unless: (1) the work has been registered in unpublished form and a second registration is now being sought to cover the first published edition, or (2) someone other than the author is identified as copyright claimant in the earlier registration, and the author is now seeking registration in his or her own name. If either of these two exceptions apply, check the appropriate box and give the earlier registration number and date. Otherwise, do not submit Form VA; instead, write the Copyright Office for information about supplementary registration or recordation of transfer of copyright ownership.

• **Changed Version:** If the work has been changed, and you are now seeking registration to cover the additions or revisions, check the third box in space 5, give the earlier registration number and date, and complete both parts of space 6.

• **Previous Registration Number and Date:** If more than one previous registration has been made for the work, give the number and date of the latest registration.

## SPACE 6: COMPILATION OR DERIVATIVE WORK

• **General Instructions:** Complete both parts of space 6 if this work is a "compilation," or "derivative work," or both, and if it is based on or incorpo-

# MORE INFORMATION

**THE COPYRIGHT NOTICE:** For published works, the law provides that a copyright notice in a specified form "shall be placed on all publicly distributed copies from which the work can be visually perceived." Use of the copyright notice is the responsibility of the copyright owner, and does not require advance permission from the Copyright Office.

• **Form of the Notice:** The required form of the notice for copies generally consists of three elements: (1) the symbol "©", or the word "Copyright", or the abbreviation "Copr."; (2) the year of first publication; and (3) the name of the owner of copyright in the work, or an abbreviation by which the name can be recognized, or a generally known alternative designation of the owner. Example: "© 1978 Samuel Marlowe." Under the statute, the year date may be omitted from the notice in cases "where a pictorial, graphic, or sculptural work, with accompanying text matter, if any, is reproduced in or on greeting cards, postcards, stationery, jewelry, dolls, toys, or any useful articles."

• **Position of the Notice:** The notice is to be affixed to the copies "in such manner and location as to give reasonable notice of the claim of copyright."

• **Errors or Omissions:** Unlike the law in effect before 1978, the new copyright statute provides procedures for correcting errors in the copyright notice, and even for curing the omission of the notice. However, a failure to comply with the notice requirements may still result in the loss of some copyright protection and, unless corrected within five years, in

rates one or more "preexisting works" that are not eligible for registration for one reason or another, works that have already been published or registered, or works that have fallen into the public domain. A "compilation" is defined as "a work formed by the collection and assembling of preexisting materials or of data that are selected, coordinated, or arranged in such a way that the resulting work as a whole constitutes an original work of authorship." A "derivative work" is "a work based on one or more preexisting works." In addition to various forms in which works may be "recast, transformed, or adapted," derivative works include works "consisting of editorial revisions, annotations, elaborations, or other modifications" if these changes, as a whole, represent an original work of authorship.

• **Preexisting Material:** If the work is a compilation, give a brief, general statement describing the nature of the material that has been compiled. Example: "Compilation of 19th Century political cartoons". **In the case of a derivative work,** identify the preexisting work that has been recast, transformed, or adapted. Examples: "Grunewald Altarpiece"; "19th Century quilt design."

• **Material Added to this Work:** The statute requires a "brief, general statement of the additional material covered by the copyright claim being registered." This statement should describe all of the material in this particular version of the work that: (1) represents an original work of authorship; (2) has not fallen into public domain; (3) has not been previously published; and (4) has not been previously registered for copyright in unpublished form. Examples: "Adaptation of design and additional artistic work"; "Reproduction of painting by photolithography"; "Additional cartographic material"; "Compilation of photographs."

## SPACES 7, 8, 9: FEE, CORRESPONDENCE, CERTIFICATION, RETURN ADDRESS

• **Deposit Account and Mailing Instructions (Space 7):** If you maintain a Deposit Account in the Copyright Office, identify it in space 7. Otherwise you will need to send the registration fee of $10 with your application. The space headed "Correspondence" should contain the name and address of the person to be consulted if correspondence about this application becomes necessary.

• **Certification (Space 8):** The application is not acceptable unless it bears the handwritten signature of the author or other copyright claimant, or of the owner of exclusive right(s), or of the duly authorized agent of such author, claimant, or owner.

• **Address for Return of Certificate (Space 9):** The address box must be completed legibly, since the certificate will be returned in a window envelope.

the complete loss of copyright. For further information about the copyright notice and the procedures for correcting errors or omissions, write to the Copyright Office.

## FORM OF DEPOSIT FOR WORKS OF THE VISUAL ARTS

**Exceptions to General Deposit Requirements:** As explained on the reverse side of this page, the statutory deposit requirements (generally one copy for unpublished works and two copies for published works) will vary for particular kinds of works of the visual arts. The copyright law authorizes the Register of Copyrights to issue regulations specifying "the administrative classes into which works are to be placed for purposes of deposit and registration, and the nature of the copies or phonorecords to be deposited in the various classes specified." For particular classes, the regulations may require or permit "the deposit of identifying material instead of copies or phonorecords," or "the deposit of only one copy or phonorecord where two would normally be required."

**What Should You Deposit?** The detailed requirements with respect to the kind of deposit to accompany an application on Form VA are contained in the Copyright Office Regulations. The following does not cover all of the deposit requirements, but is intended to give you some general guidance.

• For an unpublished work, the material deposited should represent the entire copyrightable content of the work for which registration is being sought:

• For a published work, the material deposited should generally consist of two complete copies of the best edition. Exceptions:

—For certain types of works, one complete copy may be deposited instead of two. These include greeting cards, postcards, stationery, labels, advertisements, scientific drawings, and globes.

—For most three-dimensional sculptural works, and for certain two-dimensional works, the Copyright Office Regulations require the deposit of identifying material (photographs or drawings in a specified form) rather than copies.

—Under certain circumstances, for works published in five copies or less or in limited, numbered editions, the deposit may consist of one copy or of identifying reproductions.

# APPLICATION
# FOR
# COPYRIGHT
# REGISTRATION

*for a*
*Sound Recording*

## FORM SR

UNITED STATES COPYRIGHT OFFICE
LIBRARY OF CONGRESS
WASHINGTON, D.C. 20559

---

### HOW TO APPLY FOR COPYRIGHT REGISTRATION:

- **First:** Read the information on this page to make sure Form SR is the correct application for your work.

- **Second:** Open out the form by pulling this page to the left. Read through the detailed instructions before starting to complete the form.

- **Third:** Complete spaces 1-4 of the application, then turn the entire form over and, after reading the instructions for spaces 5-9, complete the rest of your application. Use typewriter or print in dark ink. Be sure to sign the form at space 8.

- **Fourth:** Detach your completed application from these instructions and send it with the necessary deposit of the work (see below) to: Register of Copyrights, Library of Congress, Washington, D.C. 20559. Unless you have a Deposit Account in the Copyright Office, your application and deposit must be accompanied by a check or money order for $10, payable to: *Register of Copyrights.*

**WHEN TO USE FORM SR:** Form SR is the appropriate application to use for copyright registration covering a sound recording. It should be used where the copyright claim is limited to the sound recording itself, and it should also be used where the same copyright claimant is seeking to register not only the sound recording but also the musical, dramatic, or literary work embodied in the sound recording. Both published and unpublished works can be registered on Form SR.

**WHAT IS A "SOUND RECORDING"?** With one exception, "sound recordings" are works that result from the fixation of a series of musical, spoken, or other sounds. The exception is for the audio portions of audiovisual works, such as a motion picture soundtrack or an audio cassette accompanying a filmstrip; these are considered an integral part of the audiovisual work as a whole. For further information about "sound recordings" and the distinction between "sound recordings" and "phonorecords," see the reverse side of this sheet. For additional information about copyright in sound recordings, write for Circular R56.

**DEPOSIT TO ACCOMPANY APPLICATION:** An application for copyright registration must be accompanied by a deposit representing the entire work for which registration is to be made. For registration on Form SR, the following are the general deposit requirements:

*Unpublished work:* Deposit one complete phonorecord.

*Published work:* Deposit two complete phonorecords of the best edition, together with "any printed or other visually perceptible material" published with the phonorecords.

***Work first published outside the United States:*** Deposit one complete phonorecord of the work as first published.

***Contribution to a collective work:*** Deposit one complete phonorecord of the best edition of the collective work.

These general deposit requirements may vary in particular situations. For further information about the deposit requirements for sound recordings, see the reverse side of this sheet. For general information about copyright deposit, write for Circular R7.

**THE COPYRIGHT NOTICE:** For published sound recordings, the law provides that a copyright notice in a specified form "shall be placed on all publicly distributed phonorecords of the sound recording." Use of the copyright notice is the responsibility of the copyright owner and does not require advance permission from the Copyright Office. The required form of the notice for phonorecords generally consists of three elements: (1) the symbol "℗" (the letter P in a circle); (2) the year of first publication of the sound recording; and (3) the name of the owner of copyright. For example: "℗ 1978 Rittenhouse Record Co." The notice is to be "placed on the surface of the phonorecord, or on the label or container, in such manner and location as to give reasonable notice of the claim of copyright." Unlike the law in effect before 1978, the new copyright statute provides procedures for correcting errors in the copyright notice, and even for curing the omission of the notice. However, a failure to comply with the notice requirements may still result in the loss of some copyright protection and, unless corrected within five years, in the complete loss of copyright. For further information about the copyright notice, see the reverse side of this sheet. For additional information concerning the copyright notice and the procedures for correcting errors or omissions, write for Circular R3.

**DURATION OF COPYRIGHT:** For works that were created after the effective date of the new statute (January 1, 1978), the basic copyright term will be the life of the author and fifty years after the author's death. For works made for hire, and for certain anonymous and pseudonymous works, the duration of copyright will be 75 years from publication or 100 years from creation, whichever is shorter. These same terms of copyright will generally apply to works that had been created before 1978 but had not been published or copyrighted before that date. Sound recordings fixed before February 15, 1972 are not eligible for registration, but may be protected by state law. For further information about the duration of copyright, including the terms of copyrights already in existence before 1978, write for Circular R15a.

# FORM SR

UNITED STATES COPYRIGHT OFFICE

REGISTRATION NUMBER

SR          SRU

EFFECTIVE DATE OF REGISTRATION

. . . . . . . . . . . . . . . . .
Month          Day          Year

**DO NOT WRITE ABOVE THIS LINE. IF YOU NEED MORE SPACE, USE CONTINUATION SHEET (FORM SR/CON)**

| (1) Title | **TITLE OF THIS WORK:** | **NATURE OF MATERIAL RECORDED:** (Check Which) |
|---|---|---|

Catalog number of sound recording, if any . . . . . . . . . . . . . . . . . . . . . . . . . . . . . . . . .

□ Musical          □ Musical-Dramatic
□ Dramatic         □ Literary
□ Other: . . . . . . . . . . . . . . . . . . . . . . . . .
. . . . . . . . . . . . . . . . . . . . . . . . . . . . . . .

**PREVIOUS OR ALTERNATIVE TITLES:**

| (2) Author(s) | **IMPORTANT:** Under the law, the "author" of a "work made for hire" is generally the employer, not the employee (see instructions). If any part of this work was "made for hire" check "Yes" in the space provided, give the employer (or other person for whom the work was prepared) as "Author" of that part, and leave the space for dates blank. |
|---|---|

**NAME OF AUTHOR:**

**DATES OF BIRTH AND DEATH:**

Born . . . . . . . .  Died . . . . . . . .
(Year)              (Year)

1

Was this author's contribution to the work a "work made for hire"?    Yes . . . . . .    No . . . . . .

**WAS THIS AUTHOR'S CONTRIBUTION TO THE WORK:**

Anonymous?       Yes . . . . . .   No . . . . . .
Pseudonymous?    Yes . . . . . .   No . . . . . .

**AUTHOR'S NATIONALITY OR DOMICILE:**

Citizen of . . . . . . . . . . . . . . . . . } or { Domiciled in . . . . . . . . . . . . . . . . . . .
(Name of Country)                              (Name of Country)

**AUTHOR OF:** (Briefly describe nature of this author's contribution)

If the answer to either of these questions is "Yes," see detailed instructions attached.

**NAME OF AUTHOR:**

DATES OF BIRTH AND DEATH:
Born .......... Died ..........
(Year)          (Year)

Was this author's contribution to the work a "work made for hire"?    Yes .......    No ..........

**AUTHOR'S NATIONALITY OR DOMICILE:**
Citizen of .......... } or { Domiciled in ..........
(Name of Country)                    (Name of Country)

**AUTHOR OF:** (Briefly describe nature of this author's contribution)

**WAS THIS AUTHOR'S CONTRIBUTION TO THE WORK:**
Anonymous?     Yes ......    No ......
Pseudonymous?  Yes ......    No ......
If the answer to either of these questions is "Yes," see detailed instructions attached.

**NAME OF AUTHOR:**

DATES OF BIRTH AND DEATH:
Born .......... Died ..........
(Year)          (Year)

Was this author's contribution to the work a "work made for hire"?    Yes .......    No ..........

**AUTHOR'S NATIONALITY OR DOMICILE:**
Citizen of .......... } or { Domiciled in ..........
(Name of Country)                    (Name of Country)

**AUTHOR OF:** (Briefly describe nature of this author's contribution)

**WAS THIS AUTHOR'S CONTRIBUTION TO THE WORK:**
Anonymous?     Yes ......    No ......
Pseudonymous?  Yes ......    No ......
If the answer to either of these questions is "Yes," see detailed instructions attached.

**(2)**

**(3)**

**(3) Creation and Publication**

**YEAR IN WHICH CREATION OF THIS WORK WAS COMPLETED:**

Year ..........

(This information must be given in all cases)

**DATE AND NATION OF FIRST PUBLICATION:**

Date .......... .......... ..........
(Month)        (Day)        (Year)

Nation ..........
(Name of Country)

(Complete this block ONLY if this work has been published.)

**(4) Claimant(s)**

**NAME(S) AND ADDRESS(ES) OF COPYRIGHT CLAIMANT(S):**

**TRANSFER:** (If the copyright claimant(s) named here in space 4 are different from the author(s) named in space 2, give a brief statement of how the claimant(s) obtained ownership of the copyright.)

- Complete all applicable spaces (numbers 5-9) on the reverse side of this page
- Follow detailed instructions attached
- Sign the form at line 8

DO NOT WRITE HERE
Page 1 of ....... pages

| | EXAMINED BY: ........... | APPLICATION RECEIVED: | |
| | CHECKED BY: ........... | | |
| FOR COPYRIGHT OFFICE USE ONLY | CORRESPONDENCE: ☐ Yes | DEPOSIT RECEIVED: | |
| | DEPOSIT ACCOUNT FUNDS USED: ☐ | REMITTANCE NUMBER AND DATE: | |

**DO NOT WRITE ABOVE THIS LINE. IF YOU NEED ADDITIONAL SPACE, USE CONTINUATION SHEET (FORM SR/CON)**

**PREVIOUS REGISTRATION:**

(5) Previous Registration

- Has registration for this work, or for an earlier version of this work, already been made in the Copyright Office? Yes ........ No ........

- If your answer is "Yes," why is another registration being sought? (Check appropriate box)
  - ☐ This is the first published edition of a work previously registered in unpublished form.
  - ☐ This is the first application submitted by this author as copyright claimant.
  - ☐ This is a changed version of the work, as shown by line 6 of the application.

- If your answer is "Yes," give: Previous Registration Number. ........... Year of Registration. ...........

**COMPILATION OR DERIVATIVE WORK:** (See instructions)

(6) Compilation or Derivative Work

PREEXISTING MATERIAL: (Identify any preexisting work or works that the work is based on or incorporates.)

...........................................
...........................................
...........................................
...........................................

MATERIAL ADDED TO THIS WORK: (Give a brief, general statement of the material that has been added to this work and in which copyright is claimed.)

**DEPOSIT ACCOUNT:** (If the registration fee is to be charged to a Deposit Account established in the Copyright Office, give name and number of Account.)

Name: ........................................................

Account Number: ........................................................

**(7) Fee and Correspondence**

**CORRESPONDENCE:** (Give name and address to which correspondence about this application should be sent.)

Name: ........................................................

Address: ........................................................

........(City)........ ........(State)........ ........(ZIP)........ ........(Apt.)........

**(8) Certification (Application must be signed)**

**CERTIFICATION:** ✱ I, the undersigned, hereby certify that I am the: (Check one)

☐ author ☐ other copyright claimant ☐ owner of exclusive right(s) ☐ authorized agent of: ........(Name of author or other copyright claimant, or owner of exclusive right(s))........

of the work identified in this application and that the statements made by me in this application are correct to the best of my knowledge.

Handwritten signature: (X) ........................................................

Typed or printed name: ........................................................ Date: ........................

**(9) Address For Return of Certificate**

**MAIL CERTIFICATE TO**

(Certificate will be mailed in window envelope)

........(Name)........

........(Number, Street and Apartment Number)........

........(City)........ ........(State)........ ........(ZIP code)........

✱ 17 U.S.C. § 506(e): FALSE REPRESENTATION—Any person who knowingly makes a false representation of a material fact in the application for copyright registration provided for by section 409 or in any written statement filed in connection with the application, shall be fined not more than $2,500.

☆ U.S. GOVERNMENT PRINTING OFFICE : 1977   O—248-637

Nov. 1977—200,000

# HOW TO FILL OUT FORM SR

Specific Instructions for Spaces 1-4

- The line-by-line instructions on this page are keyed to the spaces on the first page of Form SR, printed opposite.
- Please read through these instructions before you start filling out your application, and refer to the specific instructions for each space as you go along.

## SPACE 1: TITLE

- **Title of this Work:** Every work submitted for copyright registration must be given a title that is capable of identifying that particular work. If the phonorecords of the work bear a title (or an identifying phrase that could serve as a title), transcribe its wording completely and exactly on the application.

If the work you are registering is an entire "collective work" (such as a compilation of previously-issued recordings), give the over-all title of the collection. If you are registering one or more individual contributions to a collective work, give the title of each contribution, followed by the title of the collection. Example: "'Perpetual Motion' in *Croatian Folk Songs and Dances*."

- **Nature of Material Recorded:** Indicate the general type or character of

## SPACE 2: AUTHORS

- **General Instructions:** First decide, after reading these instructions, who are the "authors" of this work for copyright purposes. Then, unless the work is a "collective work" (see below), give the requested information about every "author" who contributed any appreciable amount of copyrightable matter to this version of the work.

- **Note:** As explained in more detail elsewhere on this application form, Form SR may be used to apply for a single registration to cover not only a sound recording but also the musical, dramatic, or literary work embodied in that recording. As long as the copyright claimant is the same for both. If you are submitting this Form SR to cover the recorded musical, dramatic, or literary work as well as the sound recording itself, it is important for space 2 to include full information about the various authors of all of the material covered by the copyright claim, making clear the nature of each author's contribution.

- **Who is the "Author"?** Unless the work was "made for hire," the individual who actually created the work is its "author." In the case of a work made for

the works or other material embodied in the recording. The box marked "Literary" should be checked for nondramatic spoken material of all sorts, including narration, interviews, panel discussions, and training material. If the material recorded is not musical, dramatic, or literary in nature, check "Other" and briefly describe the type of sounds fixed in the recording. For example: "Sound Effects"; "Bird Calls"; "Crowd Noises".

- **Previous or Alternative Titles:** Complete this space if there are any additional titles for the work under which someone searching for the registration might be likely to look, or under which a document pertaining to the work might be recorded.

- **Name of Author:** The fullest form of the author's name should be given. If you have checked "Yes" to indicate that the work was "made for hire," give the full legal name of the employer (or other person for whom the work was prepared). You may also include the name of the employee (for example: "Music Makers Record Co., employer for hire of Lila Crane"). If the work is "anonymous" you may: (1) leave the line blank, or (2) state "Anonymous" in the line, or (3) reveal the author's identity. If the work is "pseudonymous" you may (1) leave the line blank, or (2) give the pseudonym and identify it as such (for example: "Huntley Haverstock, pseudonym"), or (3) reveal the author's name, making clear which is the real name and which is the pseudonym (for example: "Judith Barton, whose pseudonym is Madeleine Elster").

- **Dates of Birth and Death:** If the author is dead, the statute requires that the year of death be included in the application unless the work is anonymous or pseudonymous. The author's birth date is optional, but is useful as a form of identification. Leave this space blank if the author's contribution was a "work made for hire."

- **"Anonymous" or "Pseudonymous" Work:** An author's contribution to a

hire, the statute provides that "the employer or other person for whom the work was prepared is considered the author." Authorship of a sound recording may include the performance fixed in the recording, or the creative elements of the recording as such, or both.

• **What is a "Work Made for Hire"?** A "work made for hire" is defined as: (1) "a work prepared by an employee within the scope of his or her employment"; or (2) "a work specially ordered or commissioned" for certain uses specified in the statute, but only if there is a written agreement to consider it a "work made for hire."

• **Collective Work:** In the case of a collective work, such as a compilation of separately-made recordings, it is sufficient to give information about the author of the collective work as a whole.

• **Author's Identity Not Revealed:** If an author's contribution is "anonymous" or "pseudonymous," it is not necessary to give the name and dates for that author. However, the citizenship and domicile of the author **must** be given in all cases, and information about the nature of that author's contribution to the work should be included if possible.

work is "anonymous" if that author is not identified on the copies or phonorecords of the work. An author's contribution to a work is "pseudonymous" if that author is identified on the copies or phonorecords under a fictitious name.

• **Author's Nationality or Domicile:** Give the country of which the author is a citizen, or the country in which the author is domiciled. The statute requires that either nationality or domicile be given in all cases.

• **Nature of Authorship:** After the words "Author of" give a brief general statement of the nature of this particular author's contribution to the work. If you are submitting this Form SR to cover both the sound recording and the underlying musical, dramatic, or literary work, make sure that the precise nature of each author's contribution is reflected here. Examples where the authorship pertains to the recording: "Sound Recording"; "Performance and Recording"; "Recorded Reading"; "Compilation and Remixing of Sounds". Examples where the authorship relates to the underlying work: "Words and Music"; "Book and Lyrics"; "Co-author of Dialogue and Narration"; "Script of Speech". Examples where the authorship pertains to both: "Words, Music, Performance, Recording"; "Arrangement of Music and Recording"; "Compilation of Poems and Reading"

the author completed the particular version for which registration is now being sought, even if other versions exist or if further changes or additions are planned.

• **Publication:** The statute defines "publication" as "the distribution of copies or phonorecords of a work to the public by sale or other transfer of ownership, or by rental, lease, or lending"; a work is also "published" if there has been an "offering to distribute copies or phonorecords to a group of persons for purposes of further distribution, public performance, or public display." Give the full date (month, day, year) when, and the country where, publication first occurred. If first publication took place simultaneously in the United States and other countries, it is sufficient to state "U.S.A."

## SPACE 3: CREATION AND PUBLICATION

• **General Instructions:** Do not confuse "creation" with "publication." Every application for copyright registration must state "the year in which creation of the work was completed." Give the date and nation of first publication only if the work has been published.

• **Creation:** Under the statute, a sound recording is "created" when it is fixed in a phonorecord for the first time. A work is "fixed" in a phonorecord when its embodiment "is sufficiently permanent or stable to permit it to be perceived, reproduced, or otherwise communicated for a period of more than transitory duration." Where a work has been prepared over a period of time, the part of the work existing in fixed form on a particular date constitutes the created work on that date. The date you give here should be the year in which

## SPACE 4: CLAIMANT(S)

• **Name(s) and Address(es) of Copyright Claimant(s):** Give the name(s) and address(es) of the copyright claimant(s) in this work. The statute provides that copyright in a work belongs initially to the author of the work (including, in the case of a work made for hire, the employer or other person for whom the work was prepared). The copyright claimant is either the author of the work or a person or organization that has obtained ownership of the copyright initially belonging to the author.

• **Transfer:** The statute provides that, if the copyright claimant is not the author, the application for registration must contain "a brief statement of how the claimant obtained ownership of the copyright." If any copyright claimant named in space 4 is not an author named in space 2, give a brief, general statement summarizing how that claimant obtained ownership of the copyright.

# INSTRUCTIONS FOR SPACES 5-9

## SPACE 5: PREVIOUS REGISTRATION

• **General Instructions:** The questions in space 5 are intended to find out whether an earlier registration has been made for this work and, if so, whether there is any basis for a new registration. As a general rule, only one basic copyright registration can be made for the same version of a particular work.

• **Same Version:** If this version is substantially the same as the work covered by a previous registration, a second registration is not generally possible unless: (1) the work has been registered in unpublished form and a second registration is now being sought to cover the first published edition, or (2) someone other than the author is identified as copyright claimant in the earlier registration, and the author is now seeking registration in his or her own name. If either of these two exceptions apply, check the appropriate box and give the earlier registration number and date. Otherwise, do not submit Form SR; instead, write the Copyright Office for information about supplementary registration or recordation of transfer of copyright ownership.

• **Changed Version:** If the work has been changed, and you are now seeking registration to cover the additions or revisions, check the third box in space 5, give the earlier registration number and date, and complete both parts of space 6.

• **Previous Registration Number and Date:** If more than one previous registration has been made for the work, give the number and date of the latest registration.

## SPACE 6: COMPILATION OR DERIVATIVE WORK

• **General Instructions:** Complete both parts of space 6 if this work is a "compilation," "derivative work," or both, and if it is based on or incorporates one or more "preexisting works" that are not eligible for registration for one reason or another: works that have already been published and registered, or

# MORE INFORMATION

**A NOTE ON TERMINOLOGY:** The following are the meanings given to some of the terms used in the copyright statute:

• **"Works":** "Works" are the basic subject matter of copyright; they are what authors create and copyright protects. The statute draws a sharp distinction between the "work" and "any material object in which the work is embodied."

• **"Copies" and "Phonorecords":** These are the two types of material objects in which "works" are embodied. In general, **"copies"** are objects from which a work can be read or visually perceived, directly or with the aid of a machine or device, such as manuscripts, books, sheet music, film, and videotape. **"Phonorecords"** are objects embodying fixations of sounds, such as audio tapes and phonograph disks. For example, a song (the "work") can be reproduced in sheet music ("copies") or phonograph disks ("phonorecords"), or both.

• **Sound Recordings":** These are "works," not "copies" or "phonorecords." "Sound recordings" are "works that result from the fixation of a series of musical, spoken, or other sounds, but not including the sounds accompanying a motion picture or other audiovisual work."

**Example:** When a record company issues a new release, the release will typically involve two distinct "works": the "musical work" that has been recorded, and the "sound recording" as a separate work in itself. The material objects that the record company sends out are "phonorec-

recording."

**SHOULD YOU FILE MORE THAN ONE APPLICATION?** If your work consists of a recorded musical, dramatic, or literary work, and both that "work," and the sound recording as a separate "work," are eligible for registration, the application form you should file depends on the following:

• **File only Form SR if:** The copyright claimant is the same for both the musical, dramatic, or literary work and for the sound recording, and you are seeking a single registration to cover both of these "works."

• **File only Form PA (or Form TX) if:** You are seeking to register only the musical, dramatic, or literary work, not the sound recording. Form PA is appropriate for works of the performing arts; Form TX is for nondramatic literary works.

• **Separate applications should be filed on Form PA (or Form TX) and on Form SR if:**

(1) The copyright claimant for the musical, dramatic, or literary work is different from the copyright claimant for the sound recording, or

(2) You prefer to have separate registrations for the musical, dramatic, or literary work and for the sound recording.

**FORM OF COPYRIGHT NOTICE ON PHONORECORDS:**

**For sound recordings:** The copyright statute provides that, whenever a sound recording is published, a special notice of copyright (for example: "℗ 1978 Miriam Haines") "shall be placed on all publicly distributed phonorecords of the sound recording."

**For musical, dramatic, or literary works:** The copyright notice for musical, dramatic, and literary works (for example: "© 1978 George Harvey Bone") is required to appear on "all publicly distributed copies from which the work can be visually perceived." There is no requirement that the notice for musical, dramatic, or literary works be placed on phonorecords reproducing them.

---

works that have taken into the public domain, or sound recordings that were fixed before February 15, 1972. A "compilation" is defined as "a work formed by the collection and assembling of preexisting materials or of data that are selected, coordinated, or arranged in such a way that the resulting work as a whole constitutes an original work of authorship." A "derivative work" is "a work based on one or more preexisting works." In addition to various forms in which works may be "recast, transformed, or adapted," derivative works include works "consisting of editorial revisions, annotations, elaborations, or other modifications" if these changes, as a whole, represent an original work of authorship.

• **Preexisting Material:** If the work is a compilation, give a brief, general statement describing the nature of the material that has been compiled. Example: "Compilation of 1930 recordings by various Chicago jazz bands." In the case of a derivative work, identify the preexisting work that has been recast, transformed, or adapted. Example: "1945 recording by Sperryville Symphony of Bach Double Concerto."

• **Material Added to this Work:** The statute requires a "brief, general statement of the additional material covered by the copyright claim being registered." This statement should describe all of the material in this particular version of the work that: (1) represents an original work of authorship; (2) has not fallen into the public domain; (3) has not been previously published; (4) has not been previously registered for copyright in unpublished form; and (5) is not a sound recording fixed before February 15, 1972. Examples: "Recorded performances on bands 1 and 3": "Remixed sounds from original multitrack sound sources": "New words, arrangement, and additional sounds"

---

## SPACES 7, 8, 9: FEE, CORRESPONDENCE, CERTIFICATION, RETURN ADDRESS

• **Deposit Account and Mailing Instructions (Space 7):** If you maintain a Deposit Account in the Copyright Office, identify it in space 7. Otherwise you will need to send the registration fee of $10 with your application. The space headed "Correspondence" should contain the name and address of the person to be consulted if correspondence about this application becomes necessary.

• **Certification (Space 8):** The application is not acceptable unless it bears the handwritten signature of the author or other copyright claimant, or of the owner of exclusive right(s), or of the duly authorized agent of such author, claimant, or owner.

• **Address for Return of Certificate (Space 9):** The address box must be completed legibly, since the certificate will be returned in a window envelope.

Accordingly, it is now possible to register a group of contributions to periodicals, under the conditions explained below. The Copyright Office *may* decide at some future date to permit the registration of other types of related works with a single application.

If you have a group of related greeting cards, photographs, prints, dolls, fabric designs, sermons, or whatever, that do not qualify as a group of contributions to periodicals, you should contact the Copyright Office to determine whether they have adopted regulations for group registration of related works other than contributions to periodicals. If they have not, you will have to use multiple applications for copyright registration in order to register the individual works comprising the group.

A group of materials, however, can be collected into a single work. Thus, a group of photographs published as a book is a single work, even though the same photographs, if distributed separately, would be a group of individual works. The book would require a single registration, but if the photographs are distributed separately, they would require multiple registrations.

## Group of Contributions to Periodicals

You can register a claim to copyright in a group of contributions to periodicals if your works meet the following conditions: (1) all of the contributions must be by the same author; (2) the author must be an individual; (3) the works cannot have been works made "for hire"; (4) all of the works must have been *first* published as contributions to periodicals within a twelve-month period; and (5) each contribution, as first published, must have had a separate copyright notice showing the same copyright owner.

If you meet these conditions, you *may* file for copyright registration for a group of contributions to periodicals. You do not have to file for registration as a group, but a group registration will save filing fees and possibly some time in preparing the applications.

## Form GR/CP

A group registration requires the use of two copyright application forms. First, you must fill out a basic application form, that is, either Form TX, Form PA, or Form VA, depending upon the nature of the works that were contributions to periodicals. Second, you must fill out a special adjunct application, Form GR/CP (see page 80 ff.). The basic application must contain all the information required for copyright registration except the titles of the works and information concerning first publication of each work. The titles and publication dates are listed in Form GR/CP, and each contribution must be separately identified and the date of first publication separately set forth. The instructions accompanying Form GR/CP explain in detail how to complete both the basic form and Form GR/CP for group registrations.

The deposit requirement for group registration is one copy of the entire periodical issue or newspaper section in which the contribution was first published.

## Form CA—Application for Supplementary Copyright Registration

Form CA (see page 88 ff.) should be used only to correct errors or add information to an earlier copyright registration. Therefore, you must already have a copyright registration for the same work to which Form CA refers. Form CA does not replace your earlier registration, but acts as a supplement to it.

Form CA is designed to correct errors made in the original registration and to add to, update, or clarify certain information contained in original registrations. Thus, you should use Form CA when you want to do any of the following:

1. To correct any error in the information provided in the original registration. If the information was correct at the time the original application was filed, there is no error to correct.
2. To add information that could have been given in the original registration but was omitted. For example, the inadvertent omission of a previous title for the work could be corrected by using Form CA.
3. To add information that has changed since the basic registration. For example, subsequent changes in the title of the work can be added, as can changes in the copyright owner's address.
4. To clarify information contained in the basic registration. A

# FORM GR/CP

UNITED STATES COPYRIGHT OFFICE
LIBRARY OF CONGRESS
WASHINGTON, D.C. 20559

**THIS FORM:**

- Can be used solely as an adjunct to a basic application for copyright registration.

- Is not acceptable unless submitted together with Form TX, Form PA, or Form VA.

- Is acceptable only if the group of works listed on it all qualify for a single copyright registration under 17 U.S.C. § 408 (c)(2).

# ADJUNCT APPLICATION
*for Copyright Registration for a*
*Group of Contributions to Periodicals*

**WHEN TO USE FORM GR/CP:** Form GR/CP is the appropriate adjunct application form to use when you are submitting a basic application on Form TX, Form PA, or Form VA, for a group of works that qualify for a single registration under section 408(c)(2) of the copyright statute.

## WHEN DOES A GROUP OF WORKS QUALIFY FOR A SINGLE REGISTRATION UNDER 17 U.S.C. §408 (c)(2)?

The statute provides that a single copyright registration for a group of works can be made if **all** of the following conditions are met:

(1) All of the works are by the same author, who is an individual (not an employer for hire); and

(2) All of the works were first published as contributions to periodicals (including newspapers) within a twelve-month period; and

(3) Each of the contributions as first published bore a separate copyright notice, and the name of the owner of copyright in the work (or an abbreviation or alternative designation of the owner) was the same in each notice; and

(4) One copy of the entire periodical issue or newspaper section in which each contribution was first published must be deposited with the application; and

(5) The application must identity each contribution separately, including the periodical containing it and the date of its first publication.

## How to Apply for Group Registration:

*First:* Study the information on this page to make sure that all of the works you want to register together as a group qualify for a single registration.

*Second:* Turn this page over and read through the detailed instructions for group registration. Decide which form you should use for the basic registration (Form TX for nondramatic literary works; or Form PA for musical, dramatic, and other works of the performing arts; or Form VA for pictorial and graphic works). Be sure that you have all of the information you need before you start filling out both the basic and the adjunct application forms.

*Third:* Complete the basic application form, following the detailed instructions accompanying it **and the special instructions on the reverse of this page**.

*Fourth:* Complete the adjunct application on Form GR/CP and mail it, together with the basic application form and the required copy of each contribution, to: Register of Copyrights, Library of Congress, Washington, D.C. 20559. Unless you have a Deposit Account in the Copyright Office, your application and copies must be accompanied by a check or money order for $10, payable to: *Register of Copyrights.*

# ADJUNCT APPLICATION
## for
## Copyright Registration for a Group of Contributions to Periodicals

**FORM GR/CP**

UNITED STATES COPYRIGHT OFFICE

REGISTRATION NUMBER

| | | |
|---|---|---|
| TX | PA | VA |

EFFECTIVE DATE OF REGISTRATION

.......... .......... ..........
(Month)   (Day)   (Year)

FORM GR/CP RECEIVED

Page _____ of _____ pages

- Use this adjunct form only if your are making a single registration for a group of contributions to periodicals, and you are also filing a basic application on Form TX, Form PA, or Form VA. Follow the instructions, attached.

- Number each line in Part B consecutively. Use additional Forms GR/CP if you need more space.

- Submit this adjunct form with the basic application form. Clip (do not tape or staple) and fold all sheets together before submitting them.

**DO NOT WRITE ABOVE THIS LINE. FOR COPYRIGHT OFFICE USE ONLY**

**Ⓐ** **Identification of Application**

**IDENTIFICATION OF BASIC APPLICATION:**
- This application for copyright registration for a group of contributions to periodicals is submitted as an adjunct to an application filed on:
(Check which)

☐ Form TX     ☐ Form PA     ☐ Form VA

**IDENTIFICATION OF AUTHOR AND CLAIMANT:** (Give the name of the author and the name of the copyright claimant in all of the contributions listed in Part B of this form. The names should be the same as the names given in spaces 2 and 4 of the basic application.)

Name of Author: ..........................................................................................

Name of Copyright Claimant: ........................................................................

**Ⓑ** **COPYRIGHT REGISTRATION FOR A GROUP OF CONTRIBUTIONS TO PERIODICALS:** (To make a single registration for a group of works by the same individual author, all first published as contributions to periodicals within a 12-month period (see instructions), give full information about each contribution. If more space is needed, use additional Forms GR/CP.)

**Registration For Group of Contributions**

☐
Title of Contribution: . . . . . . . . . . . . . . . . . . . . . . . . . . . . . . . . . . . . . .
Title of Periodical: . . . . . . . . . . . . . . . . . . . . . Vol. . . . . No. . . . . Issue Date . . . . . . . . . Pages . . . . . . . . .
Date of First Publication: . . . . . . . . . (Month) . . . . . . (Day) . . . . . (Year) Nation of First Publication . . . . . . . . . (Country)

☐
Title of Contribution: . . . . . . . . . . . . . . . . . . . . . . . . . . . . . . . . . . . . . .
Title of Periodical: . . . . . . . . . . . . . . . . . . . . . Vol. . . . . No. . . . . Issue Date . . . . . . . . . Pages . . . . . . . . .
Date of First Publication: . . . . . . . . . (Month) . . . . . . (Day) . . . . . (Year) Nation of First Publication . . . . . . . . . (Country)

☐
Title of Contribution: . . . . . . . . . . . . . . . . . . . . . . . . . . . . . . . . . . . . . .
Title of Periodical: . . . . . . . . . . . . . . . . . . . . . Vol. . . . . No. . . . . Issue Date . . . . . . . . . Pages . . . . . . . . .
Date of First Publication: . . . . . . . . . (Month) . . . . . . (Day) . . . . . (Year) Nation of First Publication . . . . . . . . . (Country)

☐
Title of Contribution: . . . . . . . . . . . . . . . . . . . . . . . . . . . . . . . . . . . . . .
Title of Periodical: . . . . . . . . . . . . . . . . . . . . . Vol. . . . . No. . . . . Issue Date . . . . . . . . . Pages . . . . . . . . .
Date of First Publication: . . . . . . . . . (Month) . . . . . . (Day) . . . . . (Year) Nation of First Publication . . . . . . . . . (Country)

☐
Title of Contribution: . . . . . . . . . . . . . . . . . . . . . . . . . . . . . . . . . . . . . .
Title of Periodical: . . . . . . . . . . . . . . . . . . . . . Vol. . . . . No. . . . . Issue Date . . . . . . . . . Pages . . . . . . . . .
Date of First Publication: . . . . . . . . . (Month) . . . . . . (Day) . . . . . (Year) Nation of First Publication . . . . . . . . . (Country)

☐
Title of Contribution: . . . . . . . . . . . . . . . . . . . . . . . . . . . . . . . . . . . . . .
Title of Periodical: . . . . . . . . . . . . . . . . . . . . . Vol. . . . . No. . . . . Issue Date . . . . . . . . . Pages . . . . . . . . .
Date of First Publication: . . . . . . . . . (Month) . . . . . . (Day) . . . . . (Year) Nation of First Publication . . . . . . . . . (Country)

☐
Title of Contribution: . . . . . . . . . . . . . . . . . . . . . . . . . . . . . . . . . . . . . .
Title of Periodical: . . . . . . . . . . . . . . . . . . . . . Vol. . . . . No. . . . . Issue Date . . . . . . . . . Pages . . . . . . . . .
Date of First Publication: . . . . . . . . . (Month) . . . . . . (Day) . . . . . (Year) Nation of First Publication . . . . . . . . . (Country)

# PROCEDURE FOR GROUP REGISTRATION

## TWO APPLICATION FORMS MUST BE FILED

When you apply for a single registration to cover a group of contributions to periodicals, you must submit two application forms:

(1) A basic application on either Form TX, Form PA, or Form VA. It must contain all of the information required for copyright registration except the titles and information concerning publication of the contributions

(2) An adjunct application on Form GR/CP. The purpose of this form is to provide separate identification for each of the contributions and to give information about their first publication, as required by the statute.

## WHICH BASIC APPLICATION FORM TO USE

The basic application form you choose to submit should be determined by the nature of the contributions you are registering. As long as they meet the statutory qualifications for group registration (outlined on the reverse of this page), the contributions can be registered together even if they are entirely different in nature, type, or content. However, you must choose which of three forms is generally the most appropriate on which to submit your basic application:

**Form TX:** for nondramatic literary works consisting primarily of text. Examples are fiction, verse, articles, news stories, features, essays, reviews, editorials, columns, quizzes, puzzles, and advertising copy.

**Form PA:** for works of the performing arts. Examples are music, drama, choreography, and pantomimes.

**Form VA:** for works of the visual arts. Examples are photographs, drawings, paintings, prints, art reproductions, cartoons, comic strips, charts, diagrams, maps, pictorial ornamentation, and pictorial or graphic material published as advertising.

If your contributions differ in nature, indicate the form most suitable for the majority of them. However, if any of the contributions consists preponderantly of nondramatic text matter in English, you should file Form TX for the entire group. This is

## HOW TO FILL OUT THE BASIC APPLICATION FORM WHEN APPLYING FOR GROUP REGISTRATION

In general, the instructions for filling out the basic application (Form TX, Form PA, or Form VA) apply to group registrations. In addition, please observe the following specific instructions:

**Space 1 (Title):** Do not give information concerning any of the contributions in space 1 of the basic application. Instead, in the block headed "Title of this Work", state: "See Form GR/CP, attached". Leave the other blocks in space 1 blank.

**Space 2 (Author):** Give the name and other information concerning the author of all of the contributions listed in Form GR/CP. To qualify for group registration, all of the contributions must have been written by the same individual author.

**Space 3 (Creation and Publication):** In the block calling for the year of creation, give the year of creation of the last of the contributions to be completed. Leave the block calling for the date and nation of first publication blank.

**Space 4 (Claimant):** Give all of the requested information, which must be the same for all of the contributions listed on Form GR/CP.

**Other spaces:** Complete all of the applicable spaces, and be sure that the form is signed in the certification space.

## HOW TO FILL OUT FORM GR/CP

### PART A: IDENTIFICATION OF APPLICATION

• **Identification of Basic Application:** Indicate, by checking one of the boxes, which of the basic application forms (Form TX, or Form PA, or Form VA) you are filing for registration.

• **Identification of Author and Claimant:** Give the name of the individual author exactly as it appears in line 2 of the basic application, and give the name of the copyright claimant exactly as it appears in line 4. These must be the same for all of the contributions listed in Part B of Form GR/CP.

### PART B: REGISTRATION FOR GROUP OF CONTRIBUTIONS

• **General Instructions:** Under the statute, a group of contributions to periodicals will qualify for a single registration only if the application "identifies

manufacture of copies, which the statute requires to be given for certain works.

## REGISTRATION FEE FOR GROUP REGISTRATION

The fee for registration of a group of contributions to periodicals is $10, no matter how many contributions are listed on Form GR/CP. Unless you maintain a Deposit Account in the Copyright Office, the registration fee must accompany your application forms and copies. Make your remittance payable to: Register of Copyrights.

## WHAT COPIES SHOULD BE DEPOSITED FOR GROUP REGISTRATION?

The application forms you file for group registration must be accompanied by one complete copy of each contribution listed in Form GR/CP, exactly as the contribution was first published in a periodical. The deposit must consist of the entire issue of the periodical containing the contribution; or, if the contribution was first published in a newspaper, the deposit should consist of the entire section in which the contribution appeared. Tear sheets or proof copies are not acceptable for deposit.

## COPYRIGHT NOTICE REQUIREMENTS

For published works, the law provides that a copyright notice in a specified form "shall be placed on all publicly distributed copies from which the work can be visually perceived." The required form of the notice generally consists of three elements: (1) the symbol "©", or the word "Copyright", or the abbreviation "Copr." (2) the year of first publication of the work; and (3) the name of the owner of copyright in the work, or an abbreviation or alternative form of the name. For example: "© 1978 Samuel Craig"

Among the conditions for group registration of contributions to periodicals, the statute establishes two requirements involving the copyright notice:

(1) Each of the contributions as first published must have borne a separate copyright notice; and

(2) "The name of the owner of copyright in the work, or an abbreviation by which the name can be recognized, or a generally known alternative designation of the owner" must have been the same in each notice.

publication." Part B of the Form GR/CP provides lines enough to list 19 separate contributions; if you need more space, use additional Forms GR/CP. If possible, list the contributions in the order of their publication, giving the earliest first. Number each line consecutively.

• **Important:** All of the contributions listed on Form GR/CP must have been published within a single twelve-month period. This does not mean that all of the contributions must have been published during the same calendar year, but it does mean that, to be grouped in a single application, the earliest and latest contributions must not have been published more than twelve months apart. Example: Contributions published on April 1, 1978, July 1, 1978, and March 1, 1979, could be grouped together, but a contribution published on April 15, 1979, could not be registered with them as part of the group.

• **Title of Contribution:** Each contribution must be given a title that is capable of identifying that particular work and of distinguishing it from others. If the contribution as published in the periodical bears a title (or an identifying phrase that could serve as a title), transcribe its wording completely and exactly.

• **Identification of Periodical:** Give the over-all title of the periodical in which the contribution was first published, together with the volume and issue number (if any) and the issue date.

• **Pages:** Give the number of the page of the periodical issue on which the contribution appeared. If the contribution covered more than one page, give the inclusive pages, if possible.

• **First Publication:** The statute defines "publication" as "the distribution of copies or phonorecords of a work to the public by sale or other transfer of ownership, or by rental, lease, or lending"; a work is also "published" if there has been an "offering to distribute copies or phonorecords to a group of persons for purposes of further distribution, public performance, or public display." Give the full date (month, day, and year) when, and the country where, publication of the periodical issue containing the contribution first occurred. If first publication took place simultaneously in the United States and other countries, it is sufficient to state "U.S.A."

**NOTE:** The advantage of group registration is that it allows any number of works published within a twelve-month period to be registered "on the basis of a single deposit, application, and registration fee." On the other hand, group registration may also have disadvantages under certain circumstances, since infringement of a published work begins before the work has been registered, the copyright owner can still obtain the ordinary remedies for copyright infringement (including injunctions, actual damages and profits, and impounding and disposition of infringing articles). However, in that situation—where the copyright in a published work is infringed before registration is made—the owner cannot obtain special remedies (statutory damages and attorney's fees) unless registration was made within three months after first publication of the work.

further explanation of what might be regarded as an ambiguous description of the nature of the material added by a derivative work can be clarified by means of Form CA.

Form CA should *not* be used in the following situations:

1.    To register changes or additions in the content of the work. If you have changed the work and the change is copyrightable, use one of the basic application forms to register the new version of the work. If the changes to the content of the work are not copyrightable, your original registration will protect the changed work.

2.    To renew a copyright registration. Use Form RE for all copyright renewals. This form is discussed on page 111.

3.    To record changes in copyright ownership. Changes in ownership should be recorded in the Copyright Office by forwarding the original document of transfer, signed by the copyright owner, to the Copyright Office, together with the necessary recording fee.

4.    To indicate that a work previously registered as an unpublished work has now been published. You should re-register the work on the same basic application form as the work was originally registered to indicate that it has been published since registration.

5.    To ·identify anonymous and pseudonymous authors. You should record a statement identifying the author or authors, as explained on page 104.

6.    To indicate that an author has died or is still living. Again, you should record a statement with the Copyright Office indicating that the author has died or is still living. These statements are discussed on page 104.

Form CA and the Copyright Office instructions for its use follow immediately. The form requires an *exact* identification of the original certificate, and you should even include any errors that appear on the original certificate or registration. If you are correcting an error, fill out space B; if you are adding or clarifying information, fill out space C. You can do both in a single Form CA. The "Supplementary Copyright Registration Application" does not require the deposit of copies or phonorecords, but you must pay a $10 registration fee.

# APPLICATION FOR IMPORT STATEMENT

## Manufacturing Requirement

The United States Copyright law currently prohibits the importation into the United States, and the distribution of more than 2,000 copies of, nondramatic, English-language literary works by American authors. Books manufactured in Canada are exempt from this restriction. On July 1, 1982, this prohibition will automatically come to an end, but until then, failure to comply with the manufacturing requirement means that the work has no enforceable copyright.

The exceptions which allow importation of works manufactured outside the United States include, briefly stated, (1) works that are predominantly nonliterary or dramatic in nature; (2) works in languages other than English; (3) works by nationals or people domiciled in countries other than the United States; (4) works imported by the United States government, a state government, or subdivisions (but only for nonschool purposes); (5) single copies imported for personal use; (6) Braille copies; and (7) works licensed under certain conditions to foreign nationals or people living abroad.

In order to import up to 2,000 copies of a work by an American author manufactured in a country other than the United States or Canada, the copyright applicant must request an Import Statement from the Copyright Office.

## Form IS—Import Statement

The Copyright Office requires that a particular application form be used when requesting issuance of an Import Statement, namely, Form IS, reproduced with instructions on page 98 ff. You can obtain free forms simply by writing to the Copyright Office.

The Copyright Office will not issue an Import Statement unless your work is registered, but you can apply for copyright registration at the same time you apply for an Import Statement. Since it is predominantly a nondramatic literary work that requires such a

# FORM CA

UNITED STATES COPYRIGHT OFFICE
LIBRARY OF CONGRESS
WASHINGTON, D.C. 20559

### USE THIS FORM WHEN:

- An earlier registration has been made in the Copyright Office; and

- Some of the facts given in that registration are incorrect or incomplete; and

- You want to place the correct or complete facts on record.

## Application for
## Supplementary Copyright Registration

To Correct or Amplify Information Given in the
Copyright Office Record of an Earlier Registration

**What is "Supplementary Copyright Registration"?** Supplementary registration is a special type of copyright registration provided for in section 408(d) of the copyright law.

**Purpose of Supplementary Registration.** As a rule, only one basic copyright registration can be made for the same work. To take care of cases where information in the basic registration turns out to be incorrect or incomplete, the law provides for "the filing of an application for supplementary registration, to correct an error in a copyright registration or to amplify the information given in a registration."

**How to Apply for Supplementary Registration:**

**First:** Study the information on this page to make sure that filing an application on Form CA is the best procedure to follow in your case.

**Second:** Turn this page over and read through the specific instructions for filling out Form CA. Make sure, before starting to complete the form, that you have all of the detailed information about the basic registration you will need.

**Earlier Registration Necessary.** Supplementary registration can be made only if a basic copyright registration for the same work has already been completed.

**Who May File.** Once basic registration has been made for a work, any author or other copyright claimant, or owner of any exclusive right in the work, who wishes to correct or amplify the information given in the basic registration, may submit Form CA.

**Please Note:**

• Do not use Form CA to correct errors in statements on the copies or phonorecords of the work in question, or to reflect changes in the content of the work. If the work has been changed substantially, you should consider making an entirely new registration for the revised version to cover the additions or revisions.

• Do not use Form CA as a substitute for renewal registration. For works originally copyrighted between January 1, 1950 and December 31, 1977, registration of a renewal claim within strict time limits is necessary to extend the first 28-year copyright term to the full term of 75 years. This cannot be done by filing Form CA.

• Do not use Form CA as a substitute for recording a transfer of copyright or other document pertaining to rights under a copyright. Recording a document under section 205 of the statute gives all persons constructive notice of the facts stated in the document and may have other important consequences in cases of infringement or conflicting transfers. Supplementary registration does not have that legal effect.

*Third:* Complete all applicable spaces on this form, following the line-by-line instructions on the back of this page. Use typewriter, or print the information in dark ink.

*Fourth:* Detach this sheet and send your completed Form CA to: Register of Copyrights, Library of Congress, Washington, D.C. 20559. Unless you have a Deposit Account in the Copyright Office, your application must be accompanied by a check or money order for $10 payable to: *Register of Copyrights.* Do not send copies, phonorecords, or supporting documents with your application, since they cannot be made part of the record of a supplementary registration.

**What Happens When a Supplementary Registration is Made?** When a supplementary registration is completed, the Copyright Office will assign it a new registration number in the appropriate registration category, and issue a certificate of supplementary registration under that number. The basic registration will not be expunged or cancelled, and the two registrations will both stand in the Copyright Office records. The supplementary registration will have the effect of calling the public's attention to a possible error or omission in the basic registration, and of placing the correct facts or the additional information on official record. Moreover, if the person on whose behalf Form CA is submitted is the same as the person identified as copyright claimant in the basic registration, the Copyright Office will place a note referring to the supplementary registration in its records of the basic registration.

PLEASE READ DETAILED INSTRUCTIONS ON REVERSE

# FORM CA
UNITED STATES COPYRIGHT OFFICE

REGISTRATION NUMBER

| TX | TXU | PA | PAU | VA | VAU | SR | SRU | RE |
|----|-----|----|----|----|----|----|----|----|

Effective Date of Supplementary Registration

. . . . . . . . . .    . . . . . . . . .    . . . . . . . . . .
MONTH        DAY        YEAR

**DO NOT WRITE ABOVE THIS LINE—FOR COPYRIGHT OFFICE USE**

**(A)** Basic Instructions

**TITLE OF WORK:**

**REGISTRATION NUMBER OF BASIC REGISTRATION:** | **YEAR OF BASIC REGISTRATION:**

**NAME(S) OF AUTHOR(S):** | **NAME(S) OF COPYRIGHT CLAIMANT(S):**

**(B)** Correction

**LOCATION AND NATURE OF INCORRECT INFORMATION IN BASIC REGISTRATION:**

Line Number . . . . . . . . . . . . . Line Heading or Description . . . . . . . . . . . . . . . . . . . . . . . . . . . . . . . . . . . . . . . . . . . . . .

**INCORRECT INFORMATION AS IT APPEARS IN BASIC REGISTRATION:**

**CORRECTED INFORMATION:**

**EXPLANATION OF CORRECTION:** (Optional)

**LOCATION AND NATURE OF INFORMATION IN BASIC REGISTRATION TO BE AMPLIFIED:**

Line Number . . . . . . . . . . . Line Heading or Description . . . . . . . . . . . . . . . . . . . . . . . . . . . . .

**C**

**Amplification**

**AMPLIFIED INFORMATION:**

**EXPLANATION OF AMPLIFIED INFORMATION:** (Optional)

|  | EXAMINED BY: ........... | FORM CA RECEIVED |
|  | CHECKED BY: ........... | |
|  | CORRESPONDENCE ☐ YES | REMITTANCE NUMBER AND DATE |
|  | REFERENCE TO THIS REGISTRATION ADDED TO BASIC REGISTRATION ☐ YES ☐ NO | DEPOSIT ACCOUNT FUNDS USED ☐ |

FOR COPYRIGHT OFFICE USE ONLY

**DO NOT WRITE ABOVE THIS LINE: FOR COPYRIGHT OFFICE USE ONLY**

**CONTINUATION OF:** (Check which): ☐ PART B OR ☐ PART C

**(D) Continuation**

**DEPOSIT ACCOUNT:** If the registration fee is to be charged to a Deposit Account established in the Copyright Office, give name and number of Account:

Name......................................... Account Number.........................................

**(E) Deposit Account and Mailing Instructions**

**CORRESPONDENCE:** Give name and address to which correspondence should be sent:

Name ............................................................................................ Apt. No. ...............

Address ............................................................................................

(Number and Street)       (City)       (State)       (ZIP Code)

**(F)** Certification (Application must be signed)

**CERTIFICATION ✱** I, the undersigned, hereby certify that I am the: (Check one)

☐ author ☐ other copyright claimant ☐ owner of exclusive right(s) ☐ authorized agent of: ....................................
(Name of author or other copyright claimant, or owner of exclusive right(s))

of the work identified in this application and that the statements made by me in this application are correct to the best of my knowledge.

Handwritten signature: (X) ..........................................................

Typed or printed name. ............................................................

Date: ..............................................................

✱ 17 USC §506(e): FALSE REPRESENTATION—Any person who knowingly makes a false representation of a material fact in the application for copyright registration provided for by section 409, or in any written statement filed in connection with the application, shall be fined not more than $2,500.

**(G)** Address for Return of Certificate

**MAIL CERTIFICATE TO**

(Certificate will be mailed in window envelope)

.......................................................
(Name)

.......................................................
(Number, Street and Apartment Number)

.......................................................
(City)       (State)       (ZIP code)

Nov. 1977—25,000

# INSTRUCTIONS

For Completing FORM CA (Supplementary Registration)

Please read the following line-by-line instructions carefully and refer to them while completing Form CA.

## PART A: BASIC INSTRUCTIONS

• *General Instructions:* The information in this part identifies the basic registration to be corrected or amplified. Each item must agree exactly with the information as it already appears in the basic registration (even if the purpose of filing Form CA is to change one of these items).

• *Title of Work:* Give the title as it appears in the basic registration, including previous or alternative titles if they appear.

• *Registration Number:* This is a series of numerical digits, pre-

ceded by one or more letters. The registration number appears in the upper right hand corner of the certificate of registration.

• *Registration Date:* Give the year when the basic registration was completed.

• *Name(s) of Author(s) and Name(s) of Copyright Claimant(s):* Give all of the names as they appear in the basic registration.

## PART B: CORRECTION

• *General Instructions:* Complete this part **only** if information in the basic registration was incorrect at the time that basic registration was made. Leave this part blank and complete Part C, instead, if your purpose is to add, update, or clarify information rather than to rectify an actual error.

• *Incorrect Information as it Appears in Basic Registration:* Transcribe the erroneous statement exactly as it appears in the basic registration.

• *Corrected Information:* Give the statement as it should have appeared.

• **Location and Nature of Incorrect Information:** Give the line number and the heading or description of the the space in the basic registration where the error occurs (for example: "Line number 3 ... Citizenship of author").

• **Explanation of Correction (Optional):** If you wish, you may add an explanation of the error or its correction.

## PART C: AMPLIFICATION

• **General Instructions:** Complete this part if you want to provide any of the following: (1) additional information that could have been given but was omitted at the time of basic registration; (2) changes in facts, such as changes of title or address of claimant, that have occurred since the basic registration; or (3) explanations clarifying information in the basic registration.

• **Location and Nature of Information to be Amplified:** Give the line number and the heading or description of the space in the basic registration where the information to be amplified appears.

• **Amplified Information:** Give a statement of the added, updated, or explanatory information as clearly and succinctly as possible.

• **Explanation of Amplification (Optional):** If you wish, you may add an explanation of the amplification.

## PARTS D, E, F, G: CONTINUATION, FEE, MAILING INSTRUCTIONS AND CERTIFICATION

• **Continuation (Part D):** Use this space if you do not have enough room in Parts B or C

• **Deposit Account and Mailing Instructions (Part E):** If you maintain a Deposit Account in the Copyright Office, identify it in Part E. Otherwise, you will need to send the registration fee of $10 with your form. The space headed "Correspondence" should contain the name and address of the person to be consulted if correspondence about the form becomes necessary.

• **Certification (Part F):** The application is not acceptable unless it bears the handwritten signature of the author, or other copyright claimant, or of the owner of exclusive right(s), or of the duly authorized agent of such author, claimant, or owner.

• **Address for Return of Certificate (Part G):** The address box must be completed legibly, since the certificate will be returned in a window envelope.

statement, the basic registration application form to be used is Form TX.

Form IS merely requires that the work, author, and copyright claimant be identified *exactly* as is or was done in Form TX. If your work is already registered, you should also fill in the registration number and date in the boxes in the upper right-hand corner of Form IS. You must also identify the person to whom the Import Statement is to be issued. Only the copyright owner or the owner of an exclusive right in the copyright can request an Import Statement. A fee of $3 is required, but there is no deposit requirement for the Import Statement. You will, however, have to make the necessary deposit and fee payment for copyright registration in connection with the Form TX application, if you have not previously registered the work and are registering it at the same time as you apply for the statement.

The Import Statement issued by the Copyright Office must be taken to the United States Customs Service at the port of entry of the copies to be imported. Customs will admit up to 2,000 copies. If fewer than 2,000 copies are imported, Customs will notify the Copyright Office of the number imported, and the Copyright Office will then automatically issue a new statement for the balance of the 2,000 copies.

If you should import copies of a nondramatic literary work that have been manufactured in a country other than the United States or Canada in violation of the manufacturing requirements, your copyright in the work will be unenforceable, but not invalid. Moreover, the enforceability of the copyright can be reinstated by manufacturing an edition in the United States or Canada and registering a claim to copyright in the work. If you believe that your work qualifies for importation under one of the exceptions briefly described, you should contact the Copyright Information Office or legal counsel for a more complete description of these exceptions.

## ADDITIONAL FORMS AND STATEMENTS

The following are certain additional forms and statements required under the new copyright laws that you may need to know about.

## Form JB—Jukebox Recordation

The new Copyright Act gives the copyright owner of a nondramatic musical work embodied in a phonorecord the exclusive right to perform the work publicly by means of a coin-operated player, a jukebox. The law also provides, however, that operators of jukeboxes who register them with the Copyright Office can obtain a compulsory license to perform music publicly upon payment of an annual royalty fee of $8. The music's copyright owner cannot refuse to have his work on the jukeboxes once the work is recorded and distributed. Form JB is obtainable from the Copyright Office Licensing Division and is used to register the operator's jukebox and to obtain the certificate necessary for compulsory licensing. The form must be filed each year during the month of January.

## Cable Systems

Television cable systems are the subject of extensive and complex provisions under the new copyright laws. Among these provisions is the ability to obtain compulsory licenses for the public performance of works by secondary transmission. Notices and various statements must be filed with the Copyright Office to comply with the licensing requirement.

## Royalty Claims

Owners of works subject to compulsory licensing under the jukebox or cable-system provisions must file a claim each year with the Copyright Royalty Tribunal (see page 184) in order to obtain compulsory licensing fees for the use of their works. Such claims can also be made on behalf of the copyright owner by a performing rights society (such as the American Society of Composers, Authors and Publishers—ASCAP—, Broadcast Music, Inc.—BMI—, or SESAC, Inc. (formerly Society of European Stage Authors and Composers), which has an agreement with the owner for the collection of royalties. The jukebox royalty claims must be filed each year during the month of January, and cable-system royalty claims must be filed during the month of July.

**FORM IS**

UNITED STATES COPYRIGHT OFFICE
LIBRARY OF CONGRESS
WASHINGTON, D.C. 20559

# REQUEST FOR ISSUANCE OF AN IMPORT STATEMENT

*under §601 of the U.S. Copyright Law*

**Use the request form on the next page (Form IS) when:**

- You are the copyright owner of a nondramatic literary work that is subject to the manufacturing provisions of §601 of the copyright law (see below); and

- Registration for the work has already been made, or is being made now; and

- Copies of the work have been manufactured outside the United States or Canada, and you want to import up to 2,000 copies of the foreign edition into the United States under the exception in 17 U.S.C. §601(b)(2).

**WHEN TO USE THE REQUEST FORM:** Submit the form on the next page (Form IS) if you wish to import copies of a work and, because of the manufacturing provisions of the copyright law, you need an Import Statement from the Copyright Office to present to officials of the United States Customs Service.

**WHAT ARE THE "MANUFACTURING PROVISIONS"?** The copyright statute currently provides that, as a general rule, the copies of a work "consisting preponderantly of nondramatic literary material that is in the English language" be manufactured in the United States or Canada in order to be lawfully imported and publicly distributed in the United States. There are a number of exceptions to this provision, and these exceptions fall into three general categories deriving from: (1) the nature of the work; or (2) the processes used to manufacture the copies; or (3) certain facts existing at the time of importation or distribution of copies in the United States. One of the exceptions of the third type provides for the issuance of an Import Statement which will permit the importation of up to 2,000 copies of a foreign edition.

**WHAT IS AN "IMPORT STATEMENT"?** Under section 601(b)(2) of the copyright law, the manufacturing provisions do not apply "where the United States Customs Service is presented with an Import Statement issued under the seal of the Copyright Office, in which case a total of no more than 2,000 copies of any one such work shall be al-

lowed entry." Thus, by presenting a valid Import Statement to the U.S. Customs Service, you can lawfully import a maximum of 2,000 copies of a work manufactured abroad, and distribute them publicly in the United States, without affecting any rights under the copyright.

**WHEN AN IMPORT STATEMENT IS NOT NECESSARY:** An Import Statement is **not** needed as a condition for importation of copies of a foreign edition in the following cases:

(1) Where the work does not consist "preponderantly of nondramatic literary material that is in the English language"; or
(2) Where none of the processes used to manufacture the copies are covered by the manufacturing provisions. In general, the processes covered by section 601 are: (1) typesetting and plate-making (where a typographic process preceded the actual printing); (2) the making of plates by a lithographic or photoengraving process (where this was a final or intermediate step before printing); and (3) the final printing and binding processes (in all cases); or
(3) Where, in general, the author is not a U.S. citizen or domiciliary (there are some limitations and qualifications on this general exception); or
(4) Where one of the other specific exceptions in section 601(b) applies.

In all other cases, if you want to import copies of a foreign edition, you will need an Import Statement.

# REQUEST FOR ISSUANCE OF AN IMPORT STATEMENT

*under §601 of*

*the U.S. Copyright Law*

**FORM IS**

UNITED STATES COPYRIGHT OFFICE
LIBRARY OF CONGRESS
WASHINGTON, D.C. 20559

REGISTRATION NUMBER:

EFFECTIVE DATE OF REGISTRATION:

. . . . . . . . . . . . . . . . . . . . . . .
(Month)          (Day)          (Year)

DATE OF ISSUE OF
IMPORT STATEMENT:

. . . . . . . . . . . . . . . . . . . . . . .
(Month)          (Day)          (Year)

---

**(A)**

**Identifica-
tion of
Work**

**TITLE OF WORK:**

**NAME(S) OF AUTHOR(S):**

**NAME(S) OF COPYRIGHT CLAIMANT(S):**

**NOTE:** If registration has already been made for this work, give the registration number and the effective date of registration in the boxes in the upper right hand corner of this form.

**B** Designee

**ISSUE IMPORT STATEMENT TO:** (Give full name and mailing address)

Name: .................................................................................................................................................

Address: ............................................ Apt. No. ...........

(Number and Street) (City) (State) (ZIP Code)

**C** Fee and Contact

**DEPOSIT ACCOUNT:** (If the fee for issuing the Import Statement is to be charged to a Deposit Account established in the Copyright Office, give name and number of Account.)

Name: .................................................................................................................................................

Account Number: ....................................................................................................................

**PERSON TO CONTACT:** (Give name, address, and telephone number of individual who can be contacted if further information is needed.)

Name: .................................................................................................................................................

Telephone: (..........) ...................................
(Area Code)

Address: ................................................................ (Apt.) ...........

(City) (State) (ZIP Code)

**D** Certification (Request must be signed)

**CERTIFICATION OF REQUEST BY COPYRIGHT OWNER (OR AGENT OF OWNER):**

✱ By signing this request form I certify that I am the:

☐ copyright owner (as shown in the records of the Copyright Office) of the work identified in Space A

☐ duly authorized agent of the copyright owner of the work identified in Space A, whose name as shown in the records of the Copyright Office is:

....................................................................................................................................
(Name of Copyright Owner)

and that the Copyright Office is hereby authorized to issue an Import Statement to the name and address given in Space B.

Handwritten signature: (X) .................................................................................

Typewritten or printed name: ..........................................................................

Address: .................................................................................................................

Date: ......................................................................................................................

**DO NOT WRITE BELOW THIS LINE. FOR COPYRIGHT OFFICE USE ONLY**

EXAMINED BY:

CHECKED BY:

CORRESPONDENCE:
☐ Yes

DEPOSIT ACCOUNT
FUNDS USED: ☐

REQUEST RECEIVED:

REMITTANCE NUMBER AND DATE:

✱ 17 U.S.C. §506(e) FALSE REPRESENTATION—Any person who knowingly makes a false representation of a material fact in the application for copyright registration provided for by section 409, or in any written statement filed in connection with the application, shall be fined not more than $2,500.

☆ U.S. GOVERNMENT PRINTING OFFICE: 1978-261-022/7

Jan. 1978—50,000

## HOW TO REQUEST ISSUANCE OF AN IMPORT STATEMENT:

- **First:** Study the information given here to make sure that obtaining an Import Statement is the appropriate procedure to follow in your case.

- **Second:** Complete all applicable spaces on the request form (Form IS), following the line-by-line instructions. Use typewriter or print in dark ink. Be sure to sign the form at space D.

- **Third:** Detach your completed request form and send it to: Register of Copyrights, Library of Congress, Washington, D.C. 20559. Unless you have a Deposit Account in the Copyright Office, your request must be accompanied by a check or money order for $3, payable to: Register of Copyrights.

**REGISTRATION REQUIRED:** The statute provides that the Import Statement shall be issued "at the time of registration for the work under section 408 or at any time thereafter." Thus, an Import Statement can be issued only if:

- Registration for the work has already been made; or
- An application for copyright registration (on Form TX), with the necessary deposit and fee, are submitted at the same time as the request for an Import Statement. Write to the Copyright Office if you need forms and information about copyright registration.

**WHO CAN OBTAIN AN IMPORT STATEMENT:** Under the statute, the Copyright Office is authorized to issue an Import Statement to "the copyright owner or to a person designated by such owner." The "copyright owner" for this purpose is either: (1) the author of the work (including, in the case of a work made for hire, the employer or other person for whom the work was prepared), or (2) the copyright claimant

## HOW TO FILL OUT THE REQUEST FORM (FORM IS)

### SPACE A: IDENTIFICATION OF WORK

*General Instructions:* The information in this space identifies the work of which copies are to be imported under the Import Statement. If registration has already been made for the work, each item in Space A should agree with the information in the certificate of registration: the registration number and effective date of registration appearing on the certificate should be transcribed in the boxes in the upper right hand corner of Form IS. If you are applying for registration at the same time you are submitting your request for issuance of an Import Statement, make sure that the information on Form IS agrees exactly with the information in your application on Form TX; in that case the Copyright Office will supply the registration number and date when it issues the Import Statement.

*Title, Author(s), Claimant(s):* Give the title (including any previous or alternative titles) and all names as they appear in your application or certificate covering the work.

identified in the registration for the work, or (3) a person or organization that has obtained ownership of one or more exclusive rights initially owned by the author, including the exclusive right to import copies of the work into the United States. The request form must be signed by the copyright owner as shown in the records of the Copyright Office (or by that owner's duly authorized agent), and must designate the person or organization to whom the statement is to be issued.

**WHAT TO DO WITH THE IMPORT STATEMENT:** A certified Import Statement will be issued for 2,000 copies, the maximum number importable under the law. The Import Statement is a valuable document, and you should take care to preserve it from loss until you need it. The Statement should be presented to the officials of the U.S. Customs Service at the appropriate port of entry at the time of importation. If the total number of copies actually imported is less than the 2,000-copy maximum, the Customs officials will notify the Copyright Office, which will issue another Import Statement for the balance. There is no need to request an additional Import Statement in this situation, and there is no additional charge for the service.

## SPACE B: PERSON DESIGNATED TO RECEIVE IMPORT STATEMENT

Give the full name and complete mailing address of the person or organization to whom the Copyright Office will issue the certified Import Statement. This space should be completed even if the same name and address appear elsewhere on the form.

## SPACE C: FEE AND CONTACT

*Deposit Account:* If you maintain a Deposit Account in the Copyright Office, identify it in Space C. Otherwise you will need to send a fee of $3 with your request.

*Person to Contact:* Identify an individual person whom we can write to about this request, if necessary. Include that person's full address and telephone number, including area code.

## SPACE D: CERTIFICATION

The Import Statement will not be issued unless this space includes the handwritten signature of the copyright owner of the work as shown in the records of the Copyright Office (or of that owner's duly authorized agent), and includes the other identifying information called for.

---

## PRIVACY ACT ADVISORY STATEMENT
### Required by the Privacy Act of 1974 (Public Law 93-579)

AUTHORITY FOR REQUESTING THIS INFORMATION:
- Title 17 U.S.C., Sec. 601

FURNISHING THE REQUESTED INFORMATION IS:
- Voluntary

BUT IF THE INFORMATION IS NOT FURNISHED:
- It may be necessary to delay or refuse the issuance of an Import Statement
- You may be prevented from importing copies of your work under 17 U.S.C. Sec. 601(b)
- If you try to import copies without an Import Statement, they may be subject to seizure and forfeiture under 17 U.S.C. Sec. 603(c)

PRINCIPAL USES OF REQUESTED INFORMATION:
- Preparation of Import Statement
- Establishment and maintenance of a public record
- Examination of the statement for compliance with legal requirements

OTHER ROUTINE USES:
- Preparation of duplicate Import Statements, if necessary
- Public inspection and copying
- Preparation of public indexes
- Preparation of search reports upon request

## Statement of Death of an Author
## (or That the Author Is Still Living)

The Copyright Office will record statements establishing the date of death of an author or that the author is still living. As explained in Chapter 3, the duration of many copyrights is the life of the author plus fifty years. Once the author dies, the life of the copyright becomes fixed, and the date upon which the work will fall into the public domain becomes known.

A statement of an author's death can only be recorded by a person having an interest in the copyright and must identify: (1) the person filing the statement; (2) the nature of the person's interest; and (3) the source of the information as to death.

The Copyright Act further provides that after a period of seventy-five years from first publication or one hundred years from creation of a work, whichever is sooner, a presumption arises that the author has died at least fifty years earlier. In order to avoid such a presumption, a statement that the author is still living can be recorded in the Copyright Office. This statement has the same requirements as the statement of death of an author. Both statements should be accompanied by a recording fee.

## Statement Revealing the Identity of an Author

Any person having an interest in the copyright of an anonymous or pseudonymous work may record a statement with the Copyright Office identifying one or more of the authors. The statement must identify the author, the person making the statement, the nature of that person's interest in the copyright, and the source of the information upon which the statement is based.

The duration of an anonymous or pseudonymous work is the shorter of seventy-five years from first publication or one hundred years from creation, as stated in Chapter 3. A statement identifying the author of a work will change the duration to the life of the author plus fifty years. Accordingly, if an author of an anonymous or pseudonymous work lives for twenty-five years after first publication or fifty years after creation, the life of the copyright will be extended by revealing the identity of the author.

## Notice of Intention to Make Phonorecords

Compulsory licenses to make phonorecords of nondramatic musical compositions can be obtained once the copyright owner has publicly distributed phonorecords of the work. In order to obtain a compulsory license, however, the person wanting the license must serve a notice of intention to make phonorecords on the copyright owner before or within fifty days of public distribution by the potential licensee. If the owner's name and address are not identified in a Copyright Office registration or other record, it is sufficient to file the notice of intention to make phonorecords with the Copyright Office. The Copyright Office has adopted regulations about the content of the notice of intention to make phonorecords, but there are no printed forms for the notice. A filing fee of $6 is also required.

## Notice of Termination of Transfers

If you have transferred your copyright, you can terminate the transfer by serving a written notice, which meets certain conditions, upon the person to whom the license or grant was made. Only the author and certain heirs have the right to terminate a transfer or license, and the termination notice must be served within a specified time period. Termination of transfers and licenses is discussed in greater detail in Chapter 3, beginning on page 114.

In order for termination to be effective, a copy of the notice served on the person concerned must be recorded with the Copyright Office before the date of termination. The Copyright Office does not have a printed form for notices of termination, but regulations as to the content of the notice have been adopted. A recording fee of $10 plus $1 per page over six pages must also be paid when the notice is recorded in the Copyright Office.

Many of the statements, claims, and notices just listed are subject to Copyright Office regulations for their form and content. You should, therefore, obtain the current Copyright Office regulations at the time you wish to make the necessary statement, claim, or notice.

# 3 how long a copyright lasts and how to renew

## CHANGES IN COPYRIGHT DURATION UNDER THE REVISED LAW

A copyright does not last forever. There is a minor exception to that statement. To a limited degree, common-law copyright protection is still in effect and perpetual in duration for copyrightable works that are *not* fixed in a tangible medium (see page 5). The vast majority of copyrights, however, have a duration that spans a specified period of time, after which all of the exclusive rights comprising the copyright expire. When a copyright expires, others may publish, distribute, adapt, perform, and display the work without the copyright owner's consent and without paying any compensation for such use. The work falls into the public domain.

Certainly one of the most significant changes under the revised law has been the extension of the duration or life of a copyright. Prior to 1978, a copyright had two terms: an initial twenty-eight-year term, and a renewal term of twenty-eight years. Now, most copyrights will have a single term without renewal, but the single term provides a longer period of protection than the previous two terms combined.

Federal copyright protection under the old law became effective on the date the work was first published with the proper notice, or, if unpublished, on the date of copyright registration. The revised law automatically provides federal copyright protection at the time of creation, instead of the date of first publication or copyright registration. Under the new law, the period of copyright protection for works created after January 1, 1978, has been increased from a maximum term of fifty-six years to a term equal to the life of the author plus fifty years, or, for certain works, to a term equal to the shorter of seventy-five years from publication or one hundred years from creation. In addition, the new Copyright Act lengthens the duration of copyright protection for works in existence prior to 1978, so that the authors of these earlier works will also benefit.

## Duration for Works Copyrighted on or after January 1, 1978

The following conditions regarding duration of copyright apply to works copyrighted after January 1, 1978:

1.  If your work was created, that is, fixed in a tangible medium, on or after January 1, 1978, the copyright in your work will last for your lifetime plus an additional fifty years. For example, if you were thirty years old when the work was created and live to the age of seventy-five, your copyright would subsist for the forty-five years of your remaining life plus an additional fifty years, for a total of ninety-five years. The maximum duration was fifty-six years under the old law.

2.  If your work is one of joint ownership, the copyright will be effective until fifty years after the death of the *last* surviving joint author.

3.  In the case of an anonymous or pseudonymous work, and in the case of a work made "for hire," the copyright term is seventy-five years from publication or one hundred years from creation, whichever is *shorter*. Remember that you can change the authorship from anonymous and pseudonymous to a "named" author and thereby change the copyright period. If the author's identity is revealed by a statement recorded in the Copyright Office records,

then what was once an anonymous or pseudonymous work becomes a work by a known or named author and the standard "life of the author plus fifty years" term applies. Recording of a statement identifying the author with the Copyright Office is discussed in Chapter 2 on page 104.

## Duration for Works Created but Not Published or Copyrighted before January 1, 1978

If your work was created before January 1, 1978, but you had neither registered it nor published it with the proper copyright notice, it would not have been subject to federal copyright protection prior to 1978. However, the revised law provides that all such works are now protected by federal copyright as of January 1, 1978. You do not have to take any steps; copyright is now automatically extended to these works. Therefore, if you have a work in this category, the terms are the same as aforementioned: the author's life plus fifty years, or in the case of "for hire," anonymous, or pseudonymous works, seventy-five years from publication or one hundred years from creation, whichever is shorter.

Under the old law, unpublished, unregistered works would not have been accorded federal copyright protection, although they had common-law protection of potentially perpetual duration. Under the new law, this perpetual common-law protection has been eliminated for all works fixed in a tangible medium. The new law, therefore, increases the duration of copyright for most works, but shortens the life of the copyright in some. For example, under the new law, the owner of an unpublished work created ninety years ago would have the life of the copyright in the work shortened to ten years if the work was anonymous (one hundred years from creation).

Accordingly, the revised Copyright Act guarantees that all works created, but not previously published or registered, before 1978 are guaranteed a minimum of twenty-five years of copyright protection. Thus, none will expire before December 31, 2002. Also, if such an unpublished, unregistered work is published before 2003, another twenty-five years will be added to the life of the copyright. So, for example, if you have an unpublished, unregistered, anonymous, pseudonymous, or "for hire" work created in

1890, you will be entitled to copyright protection until at least 2003 (not 1990—one hundred years from creation). If you publish the work with the proper notice before 2003, you will increase the term until 2027.

If your unpublished and unregistered work was created by a named author who died in 1950, the term will extend to the year 2003 (not the year 2000—the life of the author plus fifty years). Similarly, if this work is published with the proper copyright notice before 2003, the copyright will not expire until 2027.

## Works Copyrighted and in Their First Term on January 1, 1978

Works that are copyrighted during the period from January 1, 1950, to, and including, December 31, 1977, were in their first twenty-eight-year term under the old law on January 1, 1978. These works also have had their duration of protection extended.

In order for a work to be in its first term between these dates, it must have been: published with notice during the period; *or* if it was unpublished, it must have been registered. A published work carrying the proper notice is in its first term, *even if a claim to copyright has not been registered.* If your work was originally copyrighted by publication with notice or registration between January 1, 1950, and December 31, 1977, you *must* file a renewal registration in order to have a second term of copyright protection. If you make a timely renewal application, your work will be renewed for an additional forty-seven years. Previously, the second term was for twenty-eight years, so you will now receive nineteen more years of protection under the new law. You must file for renewal within one year prior to the expiration of the original copyright term. This is very crucial; otherwise, your work will fall into the public domain, and you will irretrievably lose your copyright.

It is important to know that you cannot renew your copyright until it is first registered. If your work was published in 1976 with the proper copyright notice, the work is "copyrighted" within the meaning of the old statute and is currently in its first twenty-eight-year term. However, if it is not registered with the Copyright Office, you must first register a claim to copyright before you can renew the copyright for an additional forty-seven years. You can register the work anytime during the first twenty-eight-year term, but the renewal application can only be filed during the last year of the twenty-eight-year term. If you fail to register and renew the work, it will automatically expire at the end of the earlier of twenty-eight years from registration or first publication. Under the revised law, all copyright terms expire at the end of the calendar year (December 31) of the year of expiration. In other words, if your copyright was published with notice on March 1, 1976, it will not expire until December 31, 2004. If you fail to register a claim to copyright by December 31, 2004, and, further, to apply for a renewal registration during the year 2004, your copyright will expire at the end of the first term. If you do renew the copyright, it will not expire until December 31, 2051.

## Renewal of Copyright for Works in Their Second Term before January 1, 1978

If your work was originally copyrighted before 1950 and renewed before 1978, your copyright is in its second term, and the new law automatically extends the second term from twenty-eight to forty-seven years. This gives you a total of seventy-five years copyright protection. You do not have to apply for this extension; the renewal was automatically extended to all copyright owners in this category.

The longer copyright periods do not in any way affect works that have fallen into the public domain, nor do they restore any rights of ownership in expired copyrighted works. If your work has fallen into the public domain for any reason, nothing in the Copyright Act of 1976 revives or restores any exclusive right in the work.

# HOW TO RENEW A COPYRIGHT

The need and ability to renew a copyright applies only to people who originally copyrighted their work between January 1, 1950, and December 31, 1977. As explained in the discussion of copyright duration, only those claimants who have existing copyrights that were still in their first terms on January 1, 1978, need to and can apply for copyright renewal. Application must be made on Form RE, "Application for Renewal Registration." The Copyright Office provides the form without charge, and an example of Form RE appears on page 116 ff. The renewal fee of $6 should accompany the application, but do not send any copies or phonorecords for deposit. They are not necessary for a renewal application.

## Time Limits

There are *strict* time limits for renewal. You must file during the year prior to expiration of the first twenty-eight-year term of copyright. Your copyright term started on either the date when the work was first published with the proper notice, or the date of registration, if it was an unpublished work. To determine the date on which renewal must be made, add twenty-eight years to the exact date of publication or registration. You must have your application for renewal accepted sometime during that calendar year. For example, if you registered an unpublished work on June 22, 1958, the first term would normally expire on June 22, 1986. Under the new law, the first term is automatically extended to December 31, 1986. Your renewal application would have to be accepted and the fee received by the Copyright Office sometime between January 1, 1986, and December 31, 1986. Failure to renew during that period would cause the work to fall into the public domain, while renewal would extend the copyright until December 31, 2033.

## Who May Renew a Copyright

Renewal may be claimed *only* by the following people: (1) the author; (2) the surviving spouse or children of the deceased author; (3) the executor of the author's estate, when a will was made by the author and there are no surviving children or spouse; (4) the next of kin, in the event the author died without a will.

The right to renew the copyright is granted to the author or the deceased author's estate or heirs, regardless of who owned or owns the copyright during the original term. This means that even if the author assigned the work to another party and is not in fact the copyright owner at the time of renewal, the author or her/his heirs nevertheless have the right to renewal.

The only works that can be renewed by the copyright proprietor or owner who is not the author are: (1) a work made "for hire" (although the owner is also technically the "author"); (2) a composite work such as a periodical or encyclopedia; (3) a posthumous work, if this is a case in which the author died and there was no assignment or other contract for use of the work during the author's lifetime; (4) a work copyrighted by a corporation, but the ownership cannot be the result of an assignment or transfer by an individual author to the corporation.

## How to Complete the Renewal Application

The following information provides instruction on the correct completion of the application for copyright renewal:

1. Space 1 should be used to list the name of the renewal claimant and the basis upon which the claimant believes he is entitled to renew. As indicated above, only certain parties can renew, and the Copyright Office must determine that the renewal applicant qualifies.

2. Space 2 of Form RE requires identification of the work being renewed by *exactly* the same title as appears in the original copyright registration. As indicated on the next page, you *cannot* renew unless you have an original copyright *registration*.

Additionally, if the work being renewed is a derivative work, only the new copyrightable matter in the derivative work is renewed. The renewal of a derivative work will not renew the original or underlying work. Still further, the applicant for renewal of a derivative work is the author of the derivative work or new copyrightable subject matter, not the author of the basic work.

If the work being renewed was a contribution to a periodical or composite work, the periodical or composite work must be identified. It is possible to renew a contribution to a composite work as an independent work on a separate renewal application, even though the work was originally copyrighted with other works as a part of the larger composite work.

3. Space 3 requires identification of the author of the material being renewed. The author should be identical to that appearing in the original application for registration of the same work.

4. Space 4 requires information concerning the original copyright registration. It is not possible to renew without an original registration. *You can, however, file the original registration application and the renewal application at the same time* (within the one-year renewal period), with the necessary fees.

By way of example, a work published in 1954 with the proper copyright notice is "copyrighted" and in its first twenty-eight-year term, even though it has *never* been registered. During 1982, the work must be renewed or the copyright will permanently and irrevocably expire. If the work has not been registered by 1982, an original application for registration of a claim to copyright, together with the necessary deposit and $10 filing fee, should be filed with the Copyright Office. This original registration application can be accompanied, in 1982, but not earlier, by Form RE. If both applications are accepted by December 31, 1982, the work will be renewed. If the original application is accompanied by the renewal application, leave the "Original Registration Number" portion of space 4 blank.

Space 4 provides a place to indicate when the work was published or when it was registered, if unpublished. This information enables the Copyright Office to determine whether the Renewal Application was filed in time.

5. As discussed in Chapter 2, it is now possible to copyright a group of works published as contributions to periodicals. It is also possible to renew a group of works published as contributions to periodicals, and space 5 is provided on Form RE for such renewals. The requirements for group renewals are similar to those for group registration. All of the works must be by the same author, all must be published as contributions to periodicals, and each work must be separately identified. Additionally, however, group renewals require that the renewal claimant be the same for all works and that

all of the works must have been first published in the same calendar year. Group registration only requires first publication in the
same one-year period (for example, May 1978 to May 1979), but
since renewals can only be registered during that last year of their
first twenty-eight-year term, group renewals require groups of
works published within the same calendar year.

The remaining spaces on Form RE are identical to the equiva-
lent spaces in the basic application forms.

# TERMINATION OF TRANSFERS
# AND LICENSES

The old copyright law provided that the "author" of a work, or
certain heirs of the author, shall have the right to renew the term
of a copyrighted work for a second twenty-eight-year period. This
right to renew did not extend to the author's licensees or persons to
whom the author had assigned the copyright in the work. The
right to renew could therefore be used by the author to renegotiate
licenses and assignments at the end of the first copyright term of
twenty-eight years, presumably, when the author had a better idea
of its economic value.

Unfortunately, this statutory plan was essentially emasculated
by court decisions that permitted authors not only to assign their
works, but to assign their renewal rights.

The new Copyright Act eliminated renewal of copyrights for
works created after 1977. For these works, the old, relatively inef-
fective provision giving the author the right to renew copyright
would be meaningless. The new Copyright Act has therefore created a new right for authors—the right to terminate any licenses or
assignments of the copyright in the work.

This right to terminate transfers becomes effective thirty-five
years after the transfer or license is granted, if the license was
granted after 1977. For licenses and assignments granted before
1978, the right to terminate becomes effective fifty-six years from
the date on which the original copyright was secured by publication with notice or registration.

This means that even though you transferred your copyright to another or entered into a legally binding contract (license) for the use of your work, you can terminate that transfer or contract at certain times under certain conditions. An extremely important aspect of the termination-of-transfer provisions is that regardless of when the transfer took place, the author may elect to terminate, *even though the instrument granting the rights expressly forbids the author to terminate or purports to include an assignment of the renewal rights.*

This right to terminate can be very important. If your work has increased in value, you may want to renegotiate for more favorable terms or find a new buyer; you may want to withdraw the work from the market and/or market it yourself. Because this gives you a second chance to benefit from a successful work, you should not overlook your ability to exercise this right.

## Who May Terminate

Only the author and *certain* heirs of the author may elect to terminate. The termination of transfers and licenses will not automatically occur. The author or, if the author is dead, the author's surviving spouse, children, and grandchildren, must elect to terminate. If they do nothing, the transfer or license will stand for the full life of the copyright, unless the license or assignment provides for a shorter term. When the author dies, determining exactly who can make this election is relatively complex; this is an area in which a copyright attorney *must* be consulted.

## How to Terminate

In order to terminate a grant or license, a written notice must be served upon the grantee or licensee, or the successor to the grantee in ownership of the copyright. When a successor is involved, termination will revert the copyright to the terminating party, not any of the intermediate owners. The termination notice must be served (given to the grantee) within a time period beginning not more than ten years, nor less than two years, *before* the date on which termination is to occur. In the notice, a termination date must be set

# APPLICATION FOR
## *Renewal Registration*

**FORM RE**

UNITED STATES COPYRIGHT OFFICE
LIBRARY OF CONGRESS
WASHINGTON, D.C. 20559

## HOW TO REGISTER A RENEWAL CLAIM:

- **First:** Study the information on this page and make sure you know the answers to two questions:

  (1) What are the renewal time limits in your case?

  (2) Who can claim the renewal?

- **Second:** Turn this page over and read through the specific instructions for filling out Form RE. Make sure, before starting to complete the form, that the copyright is now eligible for renewal, that you are authorized to file a renewal claim, and that you have all of the information about the copyright you will need.

- **Third:** Complete all applicable spaces on Form RE, following the line-by-line instructions on the back of this page. Use typewriter, or print the information in dark ink.

- **Fourth:** Detach this sheet and send your completed Form RE to: Register of Copyrights, Library of Congress, Washington, D.C. 20559. Unless you have a Deposit Account in the Copyright Office, your application must be accompanied by a check or money order for $6, payable to: *Register of Copyrights*. Do not send copies, phonorecords, or supporting documents with your renewal application.

**WHAT IS RENEWAL OF COPYRIGHT?** For works originally copyrighted between January 1, 1950 and December 31, 1977, the statute now in effect provides for a first term of copyright protection lasting for 28 years, with the possibility of renewal for a second term of 47 years. If a valid renewal registration is made for a work, its total copyright term is 75 years (a first term of 28 years, plus a renewal term of 47 years). Example: For a work copyrighted in 1960, the first term will expire in 1988, but if renewed at the proper time the copyright will last through the end of 2035.

## SOME BASIC POINTS ABOUT RENEWAL:

(1) There are strict time limits and deadlines for renewing a copyright.

(2) Only certain persons who fall into specific categories named in the law can claim renewal.

(3) The new copyright law does away with renewal requirements for works first copyrighted after 1977. However, copyrights that were already in their first copyright term on January 1, 1978 (that is, works originally copyrighted between January 1, 1950 and December 31, 1977) **still have to be renewed** in order to be protected for a second term.

**TIME LIMITS FOR RENEWAL REGISTRATION:** The new copyright statute provides that, in order to renew a copyright, the renewal application and fee must be received in the Copyright Office "within one year prior to the expiration of the copyright." It also provides that all terms of copyright will run through the end of the year in which they would otherwise expire. Since all copyright terms will expire December 31st of their last year, all periods for renewal registration will run from December 31st of the 27th year of the copyright, and will end on December 31st of the following year.

To determine the time limits for renewal in your case:

(1) First, find out the date of original copyright for the work. (In the case of works originally registered in unpublished form, the date of copyright is the date of registration; for published works, copyright begins on the date of first publication.)

(2) Then add 28 years to the year the work was originally copyrighted.

Your answer will be the calendar year during which the copyright will be eligible for renewal, and December 31st of that year will be the renewal deadline. Example: a work originally copyrighted on April 19, 1957, will be eligible for renewal between December 31, 1984, and December 31, 1985.

**WHO MAY CLAIM RENEWAL:** Renewal copyright may be claimed only by those persons specified in the law. Except in the case of four specific types of works, the law gives the right to claim renewal to the individual author of the work, regardless of who owned the copyright during the original term. If the author is dead, the statute gives the right to claim renewal to certain of the author's beneficiaries (widow and children, executors, or next of kin, depending on the circumstances). The present owner (proprietor) of the copyright is entitled to claim renewal only in four specified cases, as explained in more detail on the reverse of this page.

**CAUTION:** Renewal registration is possible only if an acceptable application and fee are **received** in the Copyright Office during the renewal period and before the renewal deadline. If an acceptable application and fee are not received before the renewal deadline, the work falls into the public domain and the copyright cannot be renewed. The Copyright Office has no discretion to extend the renewal time limits.

---

**PRIVACY ACT ADVISORY STATEMENT**
Required by the Privacy Act of 1974 (Public Law 93-579)

AUTHORITY FOR REQUESTING THIS INFORMATION:
• Title 17, U.S.C., Sec. 304

FURNISHING THE REQUESTED INFORMATION IS:
• Voluntary

BUT IF THE INFORMATION IS NOT FURNISHED:
• It may be necessary to delay or refuse renewal registration

• If renewal registration is not made, the copyright will expire at the end of its 28th year

PRINCIPAL USES OF REQUESTED INFORMATION:
• Establishment and maintenance of a public record
• Examination of the application for compliance with legal requirements

OTHER ROUTINE USES:
• Public inspection and copying

• Preparation of public indexes
• Preparation of public catalogs of copyright registrations
• Preparation of search reports upon request

NOTE:
• No other advisory statement will be given you in connection with this application
• Please retain this statement and refer to it if we communicate with you regarding this application

# FORM RE

UNITED STATES COPYRIGHT OFFICE

REGISTRATION NUMBER

EFFECTIVE DATE OF RENEWAL REGISTRATION

. . . . . . . . . . . . . . . . . . . . . . . . . . . . . .
(Month)　　　　(Day)　　　　(Year)

**DO NOT WRITE ABOVE THIS LINE.　FOR COPYRIGHT OFFICE USE ONLY**

**RENEWAL CLAIMANT(S), ADDRESS(ES), AND STATEMENT OF CLAIM:** (See Instructions)

| ① Renewal Claimant(s) | | |
|---|---|---|
| 1 | Name . . . . . . . . . . . . . . . . . . . . . . . . . . . . . . . . . . . . . . . . . . . . . . . . . . . . . . . . . . . . . . . . . . . . . . . . . . . . . . . . . . . . . . . . . . .<br>Address . . . . . . . . . . . . . . . . . . . . . . . . . . . . . . . . . . . . . . . . . . . . . . . . . . . . . . . . . . . . . . . . . . . . . . . . . . . . . . . . . . . . . . . . .<br>Claiming as . . . . . . . . . . . . . . . . . . . . . . . . . . . . . . . . . . . . . . . . . . . . . . . . . . . . . . . . . . . . . . . . . . . . . . . . . . . . . . . . . . . . . . . .<br>(Use appropriate statement from instructions) | |
| 2 | Name . . . . . . . . . . . . . . . . . . . . . . . . . . . . . . . . . . . . . . . . . . . . . . . . . . . . . . . . . . . . . . . . . . . . . . . . . . . . . . . . . . . . . . . . . . .<br>Address . . . . . . . . . . . . . . . . . . . . . . . . . . . . . . . . . . . . . . . . . . . . . . . . . . . . . . . . . . . . . . . . . . . . . . . . . . . . . . . . . . . . . . . . .<br>Claiming as . . . . . . . . . . . . . . . . . . . . . . . . . . . . . . . . . . . . . . . . . . . . . . . . . . . . . . . . . . . . . . . . . . . . . . . . . . . . . . . . . . . . . . . .<br>(Use appropriate statement from instructions) | |
| 3 | Name . . . . . . . . . . . . . . . . . . . . . . . . . . . . . . . . . . . . . . . . . . . . . . . . . . . . . . . . . . . . . . . . . . . . . . . . . . . . . . . . . . . . . . . . . . .<br>Address . . . . . . . . . . . . . . . . . . . . . . . . . . . . . . . . . . . . . . . . . . . . . . . . . . . . . . . . . . . . . . . . . . . . . . . . . . . . . . . . . . . . . . . . .<br>Claiming as . . . . . . . . . . . . . . . . . . . . . . . . . . . . . . . . . . . . . . . . . . . . . . . . . . . . . . . . . . . . . . . . . . . . . . . . . . . . . . . . . . . . . . . .<br>(Use appropriate statement from instructions) | |

**②**
**Work Renewed**

**TITLE OF WORK IN WHICH RENEWAL IS CLAIMED:**

**RENEWABLE MATTER:**

**CONTRIBUTION TO PERIODICAL OR COMPOSITE WORK:**

Title of periodical or composite work: . . . . . . . . . . . . . . . . . . . . . . . . . . . . . . . . . . . . . . . . . . . . . . . . . . . . . . . . . . . . . . . . . . . . . . . . . . . . . . .

If a periodical or other serial, give: Vol. . . . . . . . . . . . . . . . . . . No. . . . . . . . . . . . . . . . . . . Issue Date . . . . . . . . . . . . . . . .

**③**
**Author(s)**

**AUTHOR(S) OF RENEWABLE MATTER:**

**④**
**Facts of Original Registration**

**ORIGINAL REGISTRATION NUMBER:**

. . . . . . . . . . . . . . . .

**ORIGINAL COPYRIGHT CLAIMANT:**

**ORIGINAL DATE OF COPYRIGHT:**

• If the original registration for this work was made in published form,
give:

DATE OF PUBLICATION: . . . . . . . . . . . . . . . . . . . . . . . . . . . . . . . . . . . . . . . . . . . . . . . . . . . . . . . . . . . . . . . .
(Month) (Day) (Year)

OR

• If the original registration for this work was made in unpublished form,
give:

DATE OF REGISTRATION: . . . . . . . . . . . . . . . . . . . . . . . . . . . . . . . . . . . . . . . . . . . . . . . . . . . . . . . . . . . . . . .
(Month) (Day) (Year)

| | RENEWAL APPLICATION RECEIVED: | FOR COPYRIGHT OFFICE USE ONLY |
|---|---|---|
| EXAMINED BY: ........<br>CHECKED BY: ........ | | |
| DEPOSIT ACCOUNT FUNDS USED:<br>☐ | REMITTANCE NUMBER AND DATE: | |

**DO NOT WRITE ABOVE THIS LINE**

**RENEWAL FOR GROUP OF WORKS BY SAME AUTHOR:** To make a single registration for a group of works by the same individual author published as contributions to periodicals (see instructions), give full information about each contribution. If more space is needed, request continuation sheet (Form RE/CON).

**⑤ Renewal for Group of Works**

| | | |
|---|---|---|
| **1** | Title of Contribution: ................................<br>Title of Periodical: ............ Vol. ..... No. ..... Issue Date .......<br>Date of Publication: ....... (Month) ....... (Day) ....... (Year) ....... Registration Number. ....... |
| **2** | Title of Contribution: ................................<br>Title of Periodical: ............ Vol. ..... No. ..... Issue Date .......<br>Date of Publication: ....... (Month) ....... (Day) ....... (Year) ....... Registration Number. ....... |
| **3** | Title of Contribution: ................................<br>Title of Periodical: ............ Vol. ..... No. ..... Issue Date .......<br>Date of Publication: ....... (Month) ....... (Day) ....... (Year) ....... Registration Number. ....... |
| **4** | Title of Contribution: ................................<br>Title of Periodical: ............ Vol. ..... No. ..... Issue Date .......<br>Date of Publication: ....... (Month) ....... (Day) ....... (Year) ....... Registration Number. ....... |
| **5** | Title of Contribution: ................................<br>Title of Periodical: ............ Vol. ..... No. ..... Issue Date .......<br>Date of Publication: ....... (Month) ....... (Day) ....... (Year) ....... Registration Number. ....... |

|   |   |
|---|---|
| 6 | Title of Contribution: ............................................................... Title of Periodical: ............................... Vol. ........ No. ........ Issue Date ........ Date of Publication: ............................................ Registration Number. ........ (Month) (Day) (Year) |
| 7 | Title of Contribution: ............................................................... Title of Periodical: ............................... Vol. ........ No. ........ Issue Date ........ Date of Publication: ............................................ Registration Number. ........ (Month) (Day) (Year) |

**DEPOSIT ACCOUNT:** (If the registration fee is to be charged to a Deposit Account established in the Copyright Office, give name and number of Account.)

Name: ...................................................

Account Number: ..........................................

**CORRESPONDENCE:** (Give name and address to which correspondence about this application should be sent.)

Name: ...................................................

Address: .................................................

................... ................... ...................
(City) (State) (ZIP)

**(6)**
**Fee and Correspondence**

**CERTIFICATION:** I, the undersigned, hereby certify that I am the: (Check one)

☐ renewal claimant      ☐ duly authorized agent of: .......................................

(Name of renewal claimant)

of the work identified in this application, and that the statements made by me in this application are correct to the best of my knowledge.

Handwritten signature: (X) ..................................

Date ...........................

Typed or printed name. ........................................

**(7)**
**Certification (Application must be signed)**

**MAIL CERTIFICATE TO**

(Certificate will be mailed in window envelope)

................................................
(Name)

................................................
(Number, Street and Apartment Number)

................... ................... ...................
(City) (State) (ZIP code)

**(8)**
**Address for Return of Certificate**

☆ U.S. GOVERNMENT PRINTING OFFICE : 1977 O—248-639

# INSTRUCTIONS FOR COMPLETING FORM RE

## SPACE 1: RENEWAL CLAIM(S)

- **General Instructions:** In order for this application to result in a valid renewal, space 1 must identify one or more of the persons who are entitled to renew the copyright under the statute. Give the full name and address of each claimant, with a statement of the basis of each claim, using the wording given in these instructions.

- **Persons Entitled to Renew:**

  A.  The following persons may claim renewal in all types of works except those enumerated in Paragraph B, below:

  1.  The author, if living. State the claim as: *the author.*
  2.  The widow, widower, and/or children of the author, if the author is not living. State the claim as: *the widow (widower) of the author* ⋯⋯⋯⋯⋯ (Name of author) and/or *the child (children) of the deceased author* ⋯⋯⋯⋯⋯ (Name of author)

  3.  The author's executor(s), if the author left a will and if there is no surviving widow, widower, or child. State the claim as: *the executor(s) of the author* ⋯⋯⋯⋯⋯ (Name of author)

  4.  The next of kin of the author, if the author left no will and if there is no surviving widow, widower, or child. State the claim as: *the next of kin of the deceased author* ⋯⋯⋯⋯⋯ *there being no will.* (Name of author)

  B.  In the case of the following four types of works, the proprietor (owner of the copyright at the time of renewal registration) may claim renewal:

  1.  Posthumous work (a work as to which no copyright assignment or other contract for exploitation has occurred during the author's lifetime). State the claim as: *proprietor of copyright in a posthumous work.*
  2.  Periodical, cyclopedic, or other composite work. State the claim as: *proprietor of copyright in a composite work.*
  3.  "Work copyrighted by a corporate body otherwise than as assignee or licensee of the individual author." State the claim as: *proprietor of copyright in a work copyrighted by a corporate body otherwise than as assignee or licensee of the individual author.* (This type of claim is considered appropriate in relatively few cases.)
  4.  Work copyrighted by an employer for whom such work was made for hire. State the claim as: *proprietor of copyright in a work made for hire.*

## SPACE 2: WORK RENEWED

- **General Instructions:** This space is to identify the particular work being renewed. The information given here should agree with that appearing in the certificate of original registration.

- **Title:** Give the full title of the work, together with any subtitles or descriptive wording included with the title in the original registration. In the case of a musical composition, give the specific instrumentation of the work.

- **Renewable Matter:** Copyright in a new version of a previous work (such as an arrangement, translation, dramatization, compilation, or work republished with new matter) covers only the additions, changes, or other new material appearing for the first time in that version. If this work was a new version, state in general what new matter upon which copyright was claimed.

- **Contribution to Periodical, Serial, or other Composite Work:** Separate renewal registration is possible for a work published as a contribution to a periodical, serial, or other composite work, whether the contribution was copyrighted independently or as part of the larger work in which it appeared. Each contribution published in a separate issue ordinarily requires a separate renewal registration. However, the new law provides an alternative, permitting groups of periodical contributions by the same individual author to be combined under a single renewal application and fee in certain cases.

  If this renewal application covers a single contribution, give all of the requested information in space 2. If you are seeking to renew a group of contributions, include a reference such as "See space 5" in space 2 and give the requested information about all of the contributions in space 5.

## SPACE 3: AUTHOR(S)

• **General Instructions:** The copyright secured in a new version of a work is independent of any copyright protection in material published earlier. The only "authors" of a new version are those who contributed copyrightable matter to it. Thus, for renewal purposes, the person who wrote the original version on which the new work is based cannot be regarded as an "author" of the new version, unless that person also contributed to the new matter.

• **Authors of Renewable Matter:** Give the full names of all authors who contributed copyrightable matter to this particular version of the work.

## SPACE 4: FACTS OF ORIGINAL REGISTRATION

• **General Instructions:** Each item in space 4 should agree with the information appearing in the original registration for the work. If the work being renewed is a single contribution to a periodical or composite work that was not separately registered, give information about the particular issue in which the contribution appeared. You may leave this space blank if you are completing space 5.

• **Original Registration Number:** Give the full registration number, which is a series of numerical digits, preceded by one or more letters. The registration number appears in the upper right hand corner of the certificate of registration.

• **Original Copyright Claimant:** Give the name in which ownership of the copyright was claimed in the original registration.

• **Date of Publication or Registration:** Give only one date. If the original registration gave a publication date, it should be transcribed here; otherwise the registration was for an unpublished work, and the date of registration should be given.

## SPACE 5: GROUP RENEWALS

• **General Instructions:** A single renewal registration can be made for a group of works if **all** of the following statutory conditions are met: (1) all of the works were written by the same author, who is named in space 3 and who is or was an individual (not an employer for hire); (2) all of the works were first published as contributions to periodicals (including newspapers) and were copyrighted on their first publication; (3) the renewal claimant or claimants, and the basis of claim or claims, as stated in space 5, is the same for all of the works; (4) the renewal application and fee are "received not more than 28 or less than 27 years after the 31st day of December of the calendar year in which all of the works were first published"; and (5) the renewal application identifies each work separately, including the periodical containing it and the date of first publication.

• **Time Limits for Group Renewals:** To be renewed as a group, all of the contributions must have been first published during the same calendar year. For example, suppose six contributions by the same author were published on April 1, 1960, July 1, 1960, November 1, 1960, February 1, 1961, July 1, 1961, and March 1, 1962. The three 1960 copyrights can be combined and renewed at any time during 1988, and the two 1961 copyrights can be renewed as a group during 1989, but the 1962 copyright must be renewed by itself, in 1990.

• **Identification of Each Work:** Give all of the requested information for each contribution. The registration number should be that for the contribution itself if it was separately registered, and the registration number for the periodical issue if it was not.

## SPACES 6, 7 AND 8: FEE, MAILING INSTRUCTIONS, AND CERTIFICATION

• **Deposit Account and Mailing Instructions (Space 6):** If you maintain a Deposit Account in the Copyright Office, identify it in Space 6. Otherwise, you will need to send the renewal registration fee of $6 with your form. The space headed "Correspondence" should contain the name and address of the person to be consulted if correspondence about the form becomes necessary.

• **Certification (Space 7):** The renewal application is not acceptable unless it bears the handwritten signature of the renewal claimant or the duly authorized agent of the renewal claimant.

• **Address for Return of Certificate (Space 8):** The address box must be completed legibly, since the certificate will be returned in a window envelope.

forth which falls within a certain five-year period. The termination notice must be signed by those having the right to terminate, and a copy of the notice *must* be recorded in the Copyright Office *before* the termination date. The author and the author's heirs cannot give away or sell their termination rights; they must first terminate the transfer and then sell the rights that revert to them.

If you believe you may have a termination right, see a copyright lawyer during the period of ten to two years before the five-year termination periods, described below.

## Termination Date

Determining when a transfer may be terminated depends upon when the license or transfer was granted. For transfers or licenses granted on or after January 1, 1978, the termination date in the written termination notice must fall within a five-year period between thirty-five years and forty years from the date of grant of the license or transfer. If the grant includes the right to publish the work, however, the termination date must fall within a five-year period starting at the earlier of thirty-five years from publication or forty years from the date of grant.

For works copyrighted, licensed, or assigned prior to January 1, 1978, the termination date must fall within a five-year period beginning at the end of fifty-six years from the date the copyright was originally secured by publication with notice or registration.

## Transfers That Cannot Be Terminated

The ability to terminate transfers and licenses does not extend to (1) works made "for hire"; (2) transfers or licenses created by wills or intestate succession; or (3) transfers or licenses made by persons other than the author, or, if the author is dead, the surviving spouse or next of kin.

The "for hire" exception is potentially dangerous for authors. Some publishers are already trying to characterize works as being made "for hire." An author's agreement to such a characterization, even though it is not true, may result in loss of the termination rights, particularly in a borderline situation.

Termination of transfers and licenses does not affect use of existing derivative works, nor does it affect transfers or licenses of foreign copyrights.

# 4 what makes a proper copyright notice

## NOTICE ESSENTIAL ON PUBLISHED WORKS

You are probably familiar in a general way with a copyright notice but have had little reason to consider its technicalities. However, if you have created a copyrightable work, copyright notice will be of considerable importance to you in its protection. In the past, failure to comply with the exact technicalities required for notice often resulted in loss of copyright. While the revised copyright laws have significantly liberalized the notice requirements and greatly reduced the risk of irrevocable loss of rights, an author must still exercise care in making certain that the proper copyright notice is used. It is quite possible to destroy your copyright by failing to place the proper copyright notice on copies and phonorecords embodying your work.

### Purpose of Notice

The purpose of the copyright notice is to indicate that the copyright owner claims exclusive rights in the work embodied in the copies or phonorecords. While the work is still unpublished, a copyright notice is not required on the copies, but once published, the copies and phonorecords must bear the proper notice in order to maintain the copyright.

## Public-Domain Materials

Not all literary, artistic, and musical works are copyrighted, and many that once were copyrighted have had the copyright expire. As a result, there is a large body of materials that is copyrightable in nature but is now in the public domain—that is, free for anyone to use.

Public-domain materials should not bear a copyright notice since no one person can claim an exclusive right in these materials. Accordingly, when a work is published without a copyright notice, there is considerable likelihood that those seeing the work will assume it is in the public domain and free for use by all. Such an assumption is not necessarily correct under the new statute. Nevertheless, absence of a copyright notice on published copies of a work tends to indicate that it is in the public domain.

Unless the owner of a copyright wants to dedicate the work to the public domain, the published copies and phonorecords containing the work should have the correct copyright notice placed in the correct location.

## What Constitutes Publication

The act of publication was critical under the old copyright law, since failure to place the proper copyright notice on a published work resulted in the work falling irrevocably into the public domain. This "old law" remains in effect for works published before January 1, 1978. If your work was published before January 1, 1978, without the correct copyright notice affixed in the correct place, you have permanently lost your copyright.

Under the new law, this catastrophic result does not automatically occur. Publication, however, still has substantial importance in many areas, including the copyright notice requirements. The new law has more clearly defined publication, making it somewhat more certain as to when it occurs. It further provides some opportunity to correct errors in, or the omission of, the copyright notice on the copies or phonorecords.

"Publication" of a work occurs upon the distribution of copies or phonorecords to the public by sale or other transfer of ownership, or by rental, lease, or lending. Offering to distribute copies or phonorecords to a group of persons for the purpose of further distribution, public performance, or public display also constitutes publication. If, however, an author publicly performs or displays a work without making copies or phonorecords available either to the public or a group—who will in turn distribute, display, or perform—the public display or performance by the author will not constitute publication. It must be remembered that the original of a work is also a "copy" or "phonorecord" so that public distribution of the original can be a publication.

## When-in-Doubt Rule

While the distinction between published and unpublished works is clearer under the new law, it can still present considerable uncertainty, particularly to the nonlawyer. Since unpublished copies and phonorecords of a work may have a copyright notice placed on them, a good when-in-doubt rule is to place the copyright notice on all copies and phonorecords, even though you may have some doubt as to whether or not a particular distribution is a "publication."

If it is unclear as to whether a particular distribution of copies or phonorecords of your work constitutes a publication, you should consider consulting a copyright attorney. If the work does not appear to justify such an expense at the time, apply the when-in-doubt rule and place the copyright notice on the copies or phonorecords. In addition, you should review the matter with legal counsel well within the first five years after the questionable publication, so you can make amendments, if necessary. The copyright statute will permit you to make corrections in the notice, but only if they are made within five years of publication.

# Exceptions to When-in-Doubt Rule

*Nondramatic musical compositions.* A notable exception to the notice-when-in-doubt rule occurs in connection with nondramatic musical compositions. There are situations in which placing a notice on copies or phonorecords would be detrimental to your purpose. Under the new copyright law, one can obtain a compulsory license to use another person's nondramatic musical compositions once phonorecords have been distributed to the public in the United States under authority of the copyright owner. If you place a copyright notice on a phonorecord, others may presume that such a public distribution has occurred, and the musical work is therefore available for use under a compulsory license—even though the work, in fact, is unpublished. Moreover, if the copyright owner has not registered a claim to copyright in the unpublished work, the person seeing the phonorecord with the notice and electing to become a compulsory licensee would not have to pay royalties to the copyright owner until the work is registered.

However, if you place a copyright notice on phonorecords of a nondramatic musical work before publication, they will be protected from the public domain, while failure to use the notice on a published phonorecord means it may enter the public domain eventually.

When a nondramatic musical composition is involved, the copyright owner should realize that following a notice-when-in-doubt rule may have drawbacks. Accordingly, consultation with a lawyer to determine whether a particular distribution will constitute publication may be a good idea.

*Works to be maintained in secrecy.* Another possible exception to the notice-when-in-doubt rule occurs in situations in which the work is being held in secrecy. If you have a work you do not want published, the copyright notice should not be placed upon the work. The copyright notice indicates that the work has been published, and may cause people to assume it can be publicly distributed or further disseminated without restriction, when in fact you want to maintain it in secrecy.

## Submissions to Publishers

Authors often want to know if a copyright notice should be on their manuscript or "demo" tape of their musical composition before submitting to a publisher. Normally, this is not necessary. The copy clearly is not being distributed to the public either directly or through a group. Instead, the copy is being forwarded to the publisher for the publisher's own use, namely, review of the work, so that the author and publisher can negotiate the possible publication of the work. The negotiations may lead nowhere, in which case the publisher is not authorized to copy or to distribute the work to others. If the author and publisher reach a full agreement and the work is published, notice would be then affixed to the published work.

However, works submitted to a publisher should be accompanied by a letter clearly stating that the work is unpublished, and that the publisher is not authorized to copy, distribute, make derivative works, or to otherwise use the work without first obtaining your written consent. Such a letter will prevent the creation of any implied licenses of use merely by reason of submission of the work to the publisher.

You should retain copies of all correspondence with the publishers, as well as an exact copy of your work as submitted. You should ask for return of your submission—although it is the practice of some publishers not to return unsolicited works. Most will return unaccepted work if you provide the return postage.

# ELEMENTS OF THE PROPER NOTICE ON PUBLISHED COPIES

There are two types of copyright notices required under the Copyright Act: the notice for copies and the notice for phonorecords of sound recordings. The word "copies" under the Copyright Act includes all types of material objects in which works may be fixed, other than phonorecords.

The proper copyright notice for works that are reproduced in visually perceptible copies must include the following three elements:

(1) the symbol ©, or the word "Copyright," or the abbreviation "Copr."; (2) the year of first publication of the work; (3) the name of the copyright owner *or* an abbreviation by which the name can be recognized *or* a generally known alternative designation of the owner.

## Copyright Symbol

The symbol © has been agreed upon by the Universal Copyright Convention—the most widely adhered to international convention on copyright laws—as an international symbol that preserves a work's copyright. This symbol, when used in combination with the year of first publication and the copyright owner's name, will be accepted by all member countries, notwithstanding the fact that the copyright laws of the individual country may specify some other form of copyright notice.

It is preferable to use the © symbol, rather than the words "Copyright" or "Copr.," in the copyright notice because of its international effect. Many countries throughout the world have no copyright-notice requirements, so failure to use © will not automatically destroy all foreign rights. (Additional discussion of international rights is on pages 145 to 147.)

You may use *both* the word "Copyright" or abbreviation "Copr." and the symbol © together in the same copyright notice, although the duplication probably adds little from the legal viewpoint. A practical argument might be that the word "Copyright" is better understood than the symbol © by nonlawyers. The symbol © and the abbreviation "Copr." are often used alone when space does not permit longer notices.

Where space permits, the following form of copyright notice for works reproduced in copies is probably the most often used in the United States:

Copyright © 1981 by John Jones

When space is limited, use of the following notice is preferred:

© 1981 John Jones

As discussed later, it may be possible to further shorten this notice by abbreviating the author's name in a recognizable manner.

The least preferred forms of notice are:

Copyright 1981 John Jones

Copr. 1981 John Jones

While these two notices are acceptable under the United States Copyright Act, they are not sufficient to preserve an author's rights in *some* countries since they do not include the international copyright-notice symbol, ©.

## Year of First Publication

The year that should appear in the copyright notice is the year in which the work was *first* published. You should not change the year in the copyright notice to correspond to the current year of distribution. Moreover, if you reprint the same work in subsequent years, you should continue to use the year of *first* publication, not the year of reprinting. The same copyright notice will protect each printing of the same version of the work, regardless of the number of printings. Some authors and publishers want to inform the public that the work has undergone several printings. You may, for example, indicate: "Tenth Printing, 1981," but this notification should be separate from the copyright notice. It can be placed on the same page as the copyright notice, but should not be part of it.

***Revised editions and derivative works.*** If you revise your work in a manner that creates new copyrightable subject matter, then you must include in the notice the year of first publication of the revised edition. Under the new law, the year of first publication of the original work before revision need not be shown in the notice.

While the year of first publication of the original work is not required on the notice under the new law, it may be included and, in most cases, this should be done. Thus, if a book was first published in 1979 and then revised to add copyrightable changes and republished in 1981, the following form of notice is recommended:

Copyright © 1979, 1981 by John Jones

If the work is revised and republished in a different medium, it might be confusing to use two years in the notice. For example, in the case of a motion picture first published in 1981 but based upon a book first published in 1979, a notice having the year of first publication of the motion picture, the derivative work, is acceptable and less confusing. Thus, the notice to be used on the motion picture would be:

Copyright © 1981 by John Jones

The credits for the motion picture normally would refer to the book and can include the copyright notice of the book, if desired.

**Collective works.** The copyright notice for a compilation should give the year of first publication of the compilation, not the year or years in which the individual contributions were first published.

**Special categories where the year is not required.** The year of first publication can be omitted from the copyright notice for a *limited* number of works specially exempted from the normal notice requirements. These are pictorial, graphic, or sculptural works reproduced in or on greeting cards, postcards, stationery, jewelry, dolls, toys, or any useful articles. The pictorial, graphic, or sculptural work may also be accompanied by text and still qualify. Omission of the year from any copies other than the specified exceptions will have the effect of making the notice improper, eventually causing the work to fall into the public domain if not corrected. While the United States Copyright Act authorizes the omission of the year from the notice on certain specified works, the Universal Copyright Convention has no such exception. So omission of the year of first publication should be avoided unless the longer notice with the year in it truly detracts from the appearance of the work.

# Name in Notice

**Copyright owner.** The third element of a proper copyright notice is the name of the copyright *owner*. This is often not the *author* of the work, although initially the author of the work will be the copyright owner. The person or business entity owning any of the exclusive rights to the work is the copyright owner. Since the copyright can be divided, one party may be the owner of the book rights, while another is the owner of the motion-picture rights. The notice on the book should show the name of the copyright owner of the book, while the notice on the motion picture would show the owner of the motion-picture rights.

**Joint owners.** If there are joint owners, the names of all owners should appear in the notice. An example would be:

Copyright © 1981 by Mary Smith and John Jones

This can be rather cumbersome if multiple owners are involved. Frequently, a business name is adopted and used on the notice. For example, if Mary Smith, John Jones, and Fred Brown have been doing business as Acme Printing Company, the notice can read:

Copyright © 1981 by Acme Printing Company

The copyright law provides that either the copyright owner's name, or an abbreviation by which the name can be recognized, or a generally known alternative designation of the owner can be used. In the above example, Acme Printing Company would be a generally known alternative designation of the owner. However, the copyright owners still have the choice of using their own names and their first names need not appear in the notice, which would read:

Copyright © 1981 by Smith, Jones, and Brown

If they have formed a separate legal entity, a partnership, or corporation and have transferred ownership of the work to the partnership or corporation, the name in the notice must be the name of the actual owner, Acme Printing Company, and not the names of the individuals.

**Abbreviated names.** When space requirements dictate, the owner's name can be abbreviated if it is recognizable from the abbreviation. One way to ensure recognition of the owner's name from the abbreviation is to repeat the owner's full name on a box or tag accompanying the work. Thus, a piece of jewelry could have the following notice stamped on it: "© A.J.C." The box or hang tag can contain the notice: "This jewelry was made by Alpha Jewelry Company of San Francisco, California." You will note that the year has been omitted from the notice, since it is jewelry.

**Works made "for hire."** The author of a work made "for hire" is the employer, and unless the ownership has been transferred, the employer will also be the copyright owner. The name of the employer, not the person who was hired to do the work, should appear in the copyright notice. The employee can be given credit as an author, but the copyright notice should show the employer as the owner.

**Assignments.** Assignments of a copyright prior to publication of copies should be reflected by using the name of the owner at the time of publication. It is not uncommon for an assignment to occur after copies have been published. Under the old law, this could have drastic consequences if the notice was not altered correspondingly. Under the revised copyright law, copies published prior to the assignment should bear the original owner's name. Copies that are distributed after the assignment has been recorded in the Copyright Office should bear the new owner's name. However, if the new owner also acquires old copies that have the original owner's name in the copyright notice, they can still be distributed. This can, of course, create the undesirable impression that the old owner still holds the copyright.

**Anonymous and pseudonymous works.** The name that appears in the copyright notice of an anonymous or pseudonymous work must be the name of the copyright owner. Even though the author is anonymous or writing under a pseudonym, the owner or copyright claimant cannot be anonymous or pseudonymous. If you write a book and want to remain anonymous, you can, for example, enter into an agreement with your publishing company to have the copyright notice in its name. The copyright notice for an anonymous work published by Acme Publishing, Inc., would be:

Copyright © 1981 by Acme Publishing, Inc.

The notice would be the same if you wrote the book under a pseudonym.

**Collective works.** Collective works, such as periodicals, anthologies, and encyclopedias are comprised of a collection of contributions that themselves each constitute independent works. The contributions to the collective work are often independently copyrighted by the separate authors. The collection or assembly of contributions itself, however, can be copyrighted separately and apart from the individual contributions.

The proper notice for a collective work must include the name of the copyright owner of the collection; the names of the copyright owners of the individual contributions should not appear in the notice for the collective work.

***Individual contributions to collective works.*** An individual contribution to a collective work may and should carry its own notice on the individual work, showing the name of the copyright owner of the contribution—not the owner of the collective work. If, however, the owner of the copyright in the individual contribution does not place a notice on the contribution, the notice for the collective work as a whole will also protect the copyright in the individual contribution. The single exception to the blanket effect of the copyright notice for collective works is found in connection with advertisements. An individual copyright notice showing the copyright owner's name must be used to preserve the copyright in an advertisement appearing in a collective work. The collective-work notice will *not* act as a blanket notice for advertisements, as it does for other contributions.

While an individual contribution to a collective work does not absolutely require an individual notice in the name of the owner of the copyright in the contribution, it is highly preferable that such a notice be employed. The blanket notice for the collective work will prevent the contributions from falling into the public domain. However, other problems may arise by not having separate notices on the individual contributions. For example, a person might reasonably assume that the owner of the collective-work copyright also owns the copyright in an individual contribution. The innocent party might further assume that the owner of the collective work has the power to license or sell the individual contribution (because the only copyright notice was in the name of the owner of the collective work). If such an arrangement is made, it would constitute innocent infringement of the copyright of the individual contribution.

## Position of Notice

Since the purpose of the notice is to inform others that the work is copyrighted and cannot be used without permission, it must be placed in a position where others could reasonably be expected to find it. Previously, the copyright law had rather technical location requirements. The notice for books, for example, had to be located on the title page or first page thereafter. Under the new law, if the notice is positioned in a location so "as to give reasonable notice of the claim of copyright," it is properly positioned. The Copyright Office has been empowered to adopt regulations (and has adopted provisional regulations) as to which locations on various types of works will automatically be regarded as meeting the notice-location requirements. However, copyright notices can be located in positions other than those specified by the Copyright Office, if, in fact, the location will result in reasonable notice.

Briefly, by way of illustration, current proposed regulations indicate that the following locations will be acceptable for books:

1. Title page
2. Page following title page
3. Either side of the front cover or page
4. Either side of the back cover or page
5. First page of main body of the work
6. Last page of main body of the work
7. Any page between the front page and main body, if there are no more than ten pages
8. Any page between the last page of the main body, and the back page, if there are no more than ten pages
9. Anywhere on a single-leaf work

Generally, the copyright notice should be affixed to copies in which the work is contained. Thus, it should not be placed upon hang tags, containers, wrappers, or other locations that are not part of the copies or permanently affixed to the copies. It is, for example, not advisable to place the copyright on a removable label or tear-out sheet that frequently will be removed from the work, giving the work the appearance of being uncopyrighted. Courts occasionally have found containers to be part of the copy, but placing the notice on the container is dangerous. Similarly, notices on easily removed gummed labels are not advised.

For fabrics, wallpaper, wrapping, and the like, a permissible position for the copyright notice is in the margin, selvage, or back of the sheet, even though the margin or selvage normally will be removed and the back covered or made inaccessible when the work is used. For repetitive designs, the notice should also be repeated at least once on each smallest commercial unit of the material which is sold.

***Position of notice on contributions to collective works.***When you make a contribution to a collective work, such as a magazine, the notice for your individual contribution can be located under the title of the contribution, adjacent to the contribution, or on the first page of the main body of the contribution. It is possible to place the notice immediately following the contribution, or, for contributions of less than twenty pages, on any page, if prominently displayed. Also, the notice can be positioned in a listing of the contributions by full title and author on the page.bearing the copyright notice for the collective work as a whole, or in the table of contents on the front or back page of the collective work.

## Visually Perceptible Copies

The copyright-notice requirements just explained apply only to works reproduced in visually perceptible copies. Tape recordings of lectures or musical compositions are examples of reproductions in which the underlying works are not visually perceptible. No notice is required for copyright protection of the lecture or musical composition. Since these examples are phonorecords of sound recordings, the phonorecord copyright notice *is required*, not for protection of the lecture or musical composition, but for protection of the particular rendition or expression of the underlying work—the sound recording.

# NOTICE ON PHONORECORDS

Phonorecords, according to the Copyright Act, are the tangible objects in which a sound recording is affixed. They require the symbol ℗ in the copyright notice, rather than the symbol © used for visually perceptible copies. Phonorecords include audiotapes, as well as discs, but they exclude sound tracks that accompany motion pictures and sound recordings that accompany other audiovisual works. Also, the fact that a work is musical in nature does not mean it requires a ℗ symbol. Sheet music and other written transcriptions are visually perceptible copies, and the correct copyright notice will include the © symbol. The ℗ symbol should be used only when sound is affixed in a phonorecord.

## Elements of the Notice

The form of notice for phonorecords contains three elements: (1) the symbol ℗ ; (2) the year of the first publication of the sound recording; (3) the name of the copyright owner.

The word "Copyright" is *not acceptable* as a proper copyright notice for sound recordings. The ℗ symbol has been recognized internationally by most of the commercially significant nations as the proper notice for sound recordings.

The year of first publication cannot be omitted from the notice for phonorecords. Moreover, the Copyright Act does not expressly state that derivative sound recordings may be published showing only the year the work was first published. It seems likely that this will be interpreted in the same manner as the notice on copies (see page 132). The safest course will be to show the date of first publication of the basic work followed by the date of first publication of the revised or derivative work.

The name of the copyright owner may include recognizable abbreviations and known alternative designations. Additionally, the Copyright Act also provides that if the phonorecord includes the producer's name on the label or container and no name appears in the notice, the producer's name will be considered as part of the notice. But, if the producer is not in fact the copyright owner, the notice may be defective, since it does not contain the copyright owner's name. The name to be included in the notice on phonorecords follows the guidelines described for the notice for copies.

The following form of notice for phonorecords is recommended: "℗ 1981 by ABC Records, Inc." For derivative works: "℗ 1980, 1981 ABC Records, Inc." Other materials are often simultaneously published with phonorecords; the cover or container for the phonorecord often contains artwork. Written materials, such as a background of the artist or record, are often contained on the inside of the album cover or in leaflets or pamphlets accompanying the phonorecord. These literary and artistic materials are not protected by the ℗ notice. They must have their own separate copyright notice, the notice required for copies (©). Thus a © notice may be employed on the album cover, while a ℗ notice appears on the record label.

Also note that the deposit requirements state that the phonorecords deposited must include the printed and artistic materials published with the phonorecord (see page 26 for the deposit requirements for sound recordings).

The copyright law specifies three acceptable locations for notice on phonorecords and then repeats the broad concept that any location giving reasonable notice is acceptable. The location requirements for the phonorecord notice are more flexible than for copies in that the notice can appear on the container. Putting the copyright notice on containers in the case of copies is not acceptable.

## Position of Notice

The acceptable locations of the copyright notice on phonorecords are: (1) on the surface of the phonorecord; (2) on the phonorecord label; (3) on the phonorecord container; (4) in such a manner and location as to give reasonable notice of the claim to copyright.

## Grouping of Elements in the Notice

The three basic elements of the copyright notice should be placed in close proximity to form an identifiable unit. Thus, the name of the copyright owner should not be separated from the symbol © or ℗ or the year of first publication.

Similarly, information other than the three basic elements of the notice should not be incorporated between the elements. Do not, for example, use the following notice:

Copyright, All Rights Reserved, 1981 by John Jones

If you want to add information to the proper notice, add it at the end, or in a separate notice spaced apart from the copyright notice. Thus the following is permissible:

Copyright © 1981 by John Jones
All Rights Reserved

Copyright © 1981 by John Jones
This book may not be reproduced
or copied without the express
written consent of John Jones.

It is preferable that the elements in the notice appear in the following order: the word "copyright" or the copyright symbol, the year of first publication, and the name of the copyright owner. Failure to use this order, however, should not endanger the copyright if all elements are present in a group that can be recognized.

# CORRECTION OF ERRORS IN NOTICE

Prior to the Copyright Act of 1976, there was little or nothing that could be done to correct errors in or the omission of the copyright notice. Under the new law, errors and omissions can be corrected for works first published after January 1, 1978; however, you cannot correct errors in or omissions of the copyright notice for works first published prior to 1978. There are a few exceptions, but generally an error or omission of the notice from copies of a work published before January 1, 1978, means the work is in the public domain.

## Omission of the Notice

Under the new law, you can even completely omit the copyright notice from published copies of a work without destroying your copyright. Omission of the copyright notice does not invalidate the copyright of a work first published in 1978 or later, if any one of the three following conditions is met:

1. The notice was omitted from only a relatively small number of the copies or phonorecords distributed to the public; or

2. Registration of the work has been made before publication or is made within five years after publication without copyright notice, and if a reasonable effort is made to add the notice to the copies or phonorecords distributed to the public after the omission has been discovered; or

3. The notice has been omitted in violation of an express requirement in writing that, as a condition of the copyright owner's authorization of the public distribution of copies or phonorecords, they bear the prescribed notice.

Thus, when the notice is omitted from a relatively small number of copies or phonorecords, the copyright is not invalidated, whether the cause of the omission was an accident, mistake, or deliberate. The key factor is whether the number of copies publicly distributed is "relatively small." Since this is a recent change in the law, it is currently uncertain where that line will be drawn.

The second set of conditions that will prevent invalidation of the copyright if the notice is omitted is that the work be registered within five years of publication, and that reasonable effort be made to add the notice to the copies distributed after discovery of the omission.

The requirement that a reasonable effort be made does not require a recall of all copies from the public. Reasonable effort to place a notice on the copies applies only to those publicly distributed after discovery of the error. However, copies that have left the publisher, but have not been publicly distributed by the distributors or bookstores, should be recalled for addition of the proper notice.

The third condition is that the copyright owner has required in a written agreement, a license agreement, that the work must have the proper notice. If the publisher, typesetter, or printer, for instance, omits the notice, contrary to the copyright owner's express written instructions, the copyright owner will not be penalized.

For most copyright owners, the chance to correct the omission of the notice by registering the work and placing a notice on the copies distributed thereafter will be the most important of the three conditions. Five years after publication, however, if the work is not registered, omission of the copyright notice from published copies is no longer correctable. The work will fall into the public domain, unless only a relatively small number has been distributed or the omission was contrary to an express written agreement requiring notice. If you have doubts as to whether you qualify to save your copyright under condition one or three, you should go ahead and register within five years of publication and add the copyright notice to the remainder of the copies to be publicly distributed.

## Effect of Omission on Innocent Infringers

While omission of the copyright notice will not automatically invalidate the copyright, it can have an adverse effect on the copyright owner. People seeing the work without copyright notice could reasonably believe that use of the work is permissible. These users are regarded as "innocent" infringers, and they are not liable for actual or statutory damages for any infringements occurring before receiving actual notice that the work is copyrighted. Moreover, the innocent infringers may, in some instances, be able to retain any profits. The courts also are empowered to permit innocent infringers to continue to use the work upon payment of a reasonable license fee. Thus, it is possible for the omission of a copyright notice from copies or phonorecords to result in compulsory licensing for innocent infringers.

It is advisable, therefore, to attempt to give actual notice as soon as possible to those who have already received copies of the work in which the notice has been omitted. Once they have actual notice, they will no longer be classified as innocent infringers. While the copies distributed to the public do not have to be recalled in order to maintain the validity of the copyright, recall and replacement for the addition of the notice is a good idea.

## Correction of Errors Other than Omission

***Name of the copyright owner.*** If the name of the copyright owner is missing from the notice, the error will be treated as though there were a complete omission of the notice; the same procedure for correction of omission of notice, as previously stated, applies.

If the name in the notice is incorrect, but present, the error will not invalidate the copyright but it should be corrected. Thus, copies distributed after discovery of the error should have the proper name in the notice. The error gives rise to the possibility of innocent infringers, who will have a sound defense if they were misled by the notice and began infringing under a purported license from the person whose name does appear. In order to eliminate potential innocent infringements, the work should be registered with the copyright office in the true owner's name, or a document should be signed by the person named in the faulty notice attesting that the true copyright owner's name is recorded in the Copyright Office.

**Year of first publication.** If the date has been completely omitted from the copyright notice, the error will be treated as a complete omission of the notice, and the same procedure for correction will apply.

If the year indicated in the copyright notice is earlier than the actual year of first publication of the work, the duration of the work will be computed from the year in the notice. For works "for hire" and anonymous and pseudonymous works, this will shorten the term of the copyright, but the copyright will not be invalidated. Works by named authors that are not "for hire" will still have a term of the life of the author plus fifty years.

If the year indicated in the copyright notice is only one year later than the year of actual first publication, the notice is not defective in any respect.

If the year indicated in the copyright notice is more than one year after the year of first publication, the error is treated as a complete omission of the notice.

**Copyright, Copr., ©, and ℗.** Failure to use at least one of the words or symbols "Copyright," "Copr.," or "©" for copies, or "℗" for phonorecords in the notice will be treated as a complete omission of the notice. The procedure for correction is the same as discussed under "Omission of Notice."

# OTHER TYPES OF NOTICES

## Notice on Works Incorporating U.S. Government Materials

A work created by the United States government is not copyrightable by the governmental agency and is free for all to use in the United States. However, when a work is published consisting preponderantly of one or more works of the U.S. government, the copyright notice must also include a statement identifying those portions of the work that are copyrightable. You must indicate what your contribution to the work is or else the effect will be the same as if you completely eliminated the copyright notice. You can define your contribution positively or negatively. For example, you may indicate, "Chapters 1 through 8 are reprinted from the U.S. government publication entitled [title]," or "Pages 55–105 and 192–360 are the subject of the copyright claimed, and the remainder of the material is reprinted from U.S. government publications." A separate copyright notice, including the three elements required, should also be placed on the work.

The additional notice concerning use of United States government materials is not required for works that include state, municipal, or local government works. These works may be the subject of copyright protection, or may not, depending upon the governmental body's policy with regard to securing copyrights.

## International Copyright Notices

The United States is a signatory to the Universal Copyright Convention, which extends copyright protection to authors of all member countries and authors who first publish a work in a member country. Copyright protection under the Universal Copyright Convention has only one requirement beyond nationality or place of first publication. When the work is published, it must contain a copyright notice that includes the following three elements: (1) the symbol ©; (2) the name of the copyright owner; and (3) the year of first publication.

The notice must be located on the work so "as to give reasonable notice of claim of copyright." While the United States permits use of the word "Copyright" and the abbreviation "Copr." in the notice, these two alternatives will not preserve your copyright under the Universal Copyright Convention. You should use the © symbol.

Many countries throughout the world have no notice requirements for copyright protection. The Universal Copyright Convention notice, including the © symbol, is only designed as an alternative to whatever notice requirements may exist in the member countries. For those countries having no notice requirements, therefore, failure to use the alternative international notice has no effect on the copyright protection afforded.

The United States is also a signatory of the Buenos Aires Convention, which has been joined by many Latin American countries. The vast majority of these countries are also members of the Universal Copyright Convention, and, accordingly, the Universal Copyright Convention notice will afford protection in most of these countries. The Buenos Aires Convention provides that a copyright obtained in one member country shall have full effect in all other member countries, provided that a statement always appears in the work indicating a "reservation of the property right." This has led to use of the expression "All Rights Reserved" below the proper Universal Copyright Convention notice. For most works the loss of rights that could result from the omission of "All Rights Reserved" will be relatively insignificant as a practical matter, but its inclusion will preserve the Buenos Aires rights.

There is a further major international copyright convention to which the United States has not become a signatory, namely, the Berne Convention. The Berne Convention affords copyright protection to nationals of member countries and to those first or simultaneously publishing in a member country. Since Canada and the United Kingdom are Berne members, this has led to simultaneous publication in the United States and Canada or the United Kingdom (within thirty days).

As additional countries join the Universal Copyright Convention, simultaneous publication is less desirable. The vast majority of commercially significant countries are members of the Universal Copyright Convention.

## Library of Congress Catalog Card Number

The Library of Congress Catalog Card Number may be obtained upon application to the Library of Congress. This notice is neither required for copyright protection nor affects it. A Library of Congress Catalog Card Number placed on your work may give you several advantages. Since some people use this source as a means of locating works of potential interest, it may provide marketing contacts. Also, your work is listed free of charge in the National Union Catalog, used by librarians and others to identify publications they may be interested in ordering.

There is no fee to obtain a Library of Congress Catalog Card Number. If you wish to use it, you should apply for your number well in advance of your printing schedule so that it can be printed on the copies.

The Library of Congress Catalog Card Number is not part of the copyright notice. It may be placed on the same page as the copyright notice, but it should appear in a separate area. The notice may read simply, "Library of Congress Catalog Number 81-12345."

The numbers are assigned by the Cataloging in Publication Office of the Processing Department (CIP), which operates independently of the Copyright Office. If you wish to apply, write to: Chief of CIP Office, Library of Congress, Washington, D.C. 20540. You should ask for the application for a Library of Congress Catalog Card Number, which requires the following information: title, author's name, edition number, year of publication, place of publication, year in which work will be copyrighted, whether or not it contains a musical score, and number of pages.

# 5 questions and answers on copyright

This section will familiarize you with some of the basic principles of the copyright law by means of a question and answer format. Copyright registration and use of the proper copyright notice are examined in previous sections on a how-to-do-it basis. This portion of the book is *not* intended to enable the reader to use a self-help approach. While covering a number of subjects and many frequently asked questions, no attempt has been made to be totally inclusive. It should, however, give you a better understanding of your rights as a copyright owner.

Unless indicated to the contrary, the answers assume that the facts in the questions occurred after January 1, 1978, the effective date of most of the provisions of the new Copyright Act. You should be aware that in some instances different answers would be required for pre-1978 circumstances.

### At what point do I have a copyright—on creation, publication, or registration?

Under the new law, you have a copyright upon creation of your work. Creation occurs when the work is fixed in a tangible medium. Even without publication or copyright registration, federal copyright protection begins from the time you put your work into tangible form. Under the old law, publication was the pivotal act of copyright. Under the revised law, the emphasis is upon creation.

### What can I do with my copyright?

You can sell any or all of the exclusive rights, license their use, bequeath them, give them away, or mortgage them. You can exercise substantially the same control over the use of any of the exclusive, intangible property rights comprising the copyright as you could over a tangible piece of personal property.

### Is there copyright protection for a work that is never fixed in a tangible medium?

You cannot copyright an idea. Federal copyright protection extends only to those works that are tangible forms of expression. Usually, but not always, the expression of an idea will require fixation in a tangible medium. Choreography, music played by ear, pantomimes, and speeches are copyrightable works that can be expressed without fixation in a tangible medium. These are examples of the few kinds of works that are still protected under the common law of copyright. If they are reduced to a tangible form, they will automatically be subject to copyright under the Copyright Act.

## COPYRIGHT—A SERIES OF EXCLUSIVE RIGHTS

Copyright is not merely the right to control the copying of a work; instead, it is a series of exclusive rights possessed by the copyright owner. The following questions and answers examine the scope of these exclusive rights.

### What is a copyright?

A copyright is a series of exclusive, personal property rights granted for a limited period of time to the author of a literary, musical, dramatic, artistic, or audible original work. Federal copyright exists only when the work has been fixed in a tangible medium. The exclusive rights granted to the author include the right to prohibit others from reproducing (copying), adapting (making derivative works), distributing, performing, or displaying the work.

### Does a copyright also protect the tangible property—for example, a painting—that I have created, or only the rights to its use?

The original work, for example, the painting, is also considered to be a "copy" and is protected by copyright. However, the tangible, physical object (the painting) and the intangible copyright relating to the use of the painting are two different types of personal property, which may be separately disposed of or used. If you sell the painting, the copyright does not automatically go to the purchaser. You can, for example, sell the painting and retain copyright ownership, thus placing yourself in a position to prohibit the new owner from making copies. Or, conversely, you can keep the original work of art and transfer your copyright ownership to another.

### If I sell the original work but do not transfer my copyright, can I still reproduce or otherwise use the work?

Yes, you may continue to exercise all the rights to your work that have not been expressly transferred in writing, whether or not you own the original. However, if you need access to the original work—for example, to make copies—you should reserve that right by contract. It is recommended that you see an attorney in order to ensure that those rights which you want to preserve will be retained.

### Is a copyright granted only to the author of a work?

Yes, the author can transfer ownership of the copyright before or after registration, but initially the rights automatically come into existence and are owned by the author upon creation of the work. There is a situation in which the creator of the work is not the "author." When an employee creates a work during the course of employment, the employer will be legally considered to be the "author" of a work made "for hire." The copyright automatically is owned by the "author," namely, the employer, who possesses all of the exclusive rights comprising the copyright even though the employee created the work.

### What is the right to reproduce?

The right to reproduce is the right to prohibit others from making copies or phonorecords of your work through any method of reproduction applicable to the particular work. Printing, photocopying, mimeographing, taping, and even copying in handwriting will constitute reproduction of a work. Reproduction requires fixation in a tangible, intelligible form.

## What is the right of distribution?

The right of distribution allows the author to control the distribution of copies or phonorecords embodying the work; this includes the right to publicly distribute copies or phonorecords—the right to publish the work. After the first distribution of a particular copy or phonorecord, however, that copy or phonorecord can be redistributed without the author's consent. Once a person becomes the owner of a lawfully made copy, he or she can sell or otherwise part with possession of that particular copy without the copyright owner's consent or permission. If you sell copies of your book to a bookstore or library, the bookstore or library is free to sell, lend, or give away those copies to whomever they wish, without the necessity of seeking authorization to further distribute the work from the copyright owner. In other words, after your distribution of a particular copy, you relinquish your right to control distribution of that copy, but you do not relinquish the right to control the distribution of subsequent copies.

## What is the right of public performance?

This right generally applies to the presentation of audible and visual works to a public audience, an audience consisting of more than just family members or social acquaintances. Your copyright includes the exclusive right to prohibit others from giving public performances of your work. No one else can perform the work publicly without your consent, although there are certain exceptions for governmental, educational, religious, and nonprofit performances. (See Chapter 6.)

## What should I do if I want to perform someone else's work?

If you perform someone else's work in public, you must obtain the copyright owner's consent. If you are performing the work in private, no consent is required. If you want to perform the work for the purpose of making and distributing phonorecords, you must obtain the copyright owner's consent or qualify for and obtain a compulsory license, if it is a musical work. Unauthorized public performance is a copyright infringement. You should contact the copyright owner, usually, the author or publisher. If a musical work is involved, you can often obtain consent by contacting ASCAP, BMI, or other professional performing rights organizations (see page 182).

### What is the right to publicly display?

This applies to paintings, photographs, statuary, other visual arts, and can include musical and literary works. Like the right of public performance, the right to prohibit others from publicly displaying your work includes the right to control the first and subsequent displays of a given copy of the work. While the sale of the physical object—for example, a painting—does not automatically transfer the copyright, the Copyright Act provides an exception that automatically grants to the purchaser of the work the right to display the work. The owner of a lawfully made copy, including the original, can publicly display that copy.

### What is the right to make adaptations or derivative works?

An adaptation, usually referred to as a derivative work, is a work based upon one or more preexisting works. It can be a modification, abridgment, condensation, translation, elaboration, compilation, editorial revision, annotation, adaption, or other form of transformation of the original work. You have the right to prohibit others from using your work to make derivative works without your consent. However, in connection with musical compositions, once you have publicly distributed phonorecords of your composition, others can re-record the work and make new musical arrangements under compulsory licensing provisions in the copyright law—as long as they do not change the basic melody or fundamental character of the work.

## PUBLICATION

Publication is discussed in Chapter 4 in connection with placement of the proper copyright notice on published works. This section briefly highlights the general principles of publication and answers questions regarding what constitutes publication in specific situations.

## What is the effect of publication upon copyright?

Publication, even though it is no longer necessary for copyright, still has very important effects. If the distribution or use of your work constitutes a publication but occurs without proper copyright notice, you may irretrievably lose the copyright that automatically came into existence upon creation of your work. It is, therefore, crucial that you are aware of what constitutes publication, and that you carefully conform to the copyright-notice requirements.

## What constitutes publication?

Publication occurs when copies or phonorecords are distributed to the public by sale or other transfer of ownership or by rental, lease, or lending. Publication also occurs if copies are offered to a group of persons for further distribution, public performance, or public display. In most cases, publication is an intentional act that will be easy to recognize, such as the publication of a book by the public distribution of copies. Problems can arise, however, when a less formal means of publication occurs, particularly if the publication occurs without the proper copyright notice on the copies or phonorecords.

## How many copies or phonorecords must be distributed to constitute publication?

It is not the number of copies distributed but the type of distribution that will determine whether publication has taken place. For example, one copy of a typewritten manuscript placed in a public library, where anyone can read it, is a publication, even though no one might actually read it. On the other hand, you can distribute twenty-five, or even more, copies to selected people under conditions of restricted use, and this distribution will not constitute a publication. Therefore, you must be careful as to how you circulate your work prior to a traditional, clearly recognizable publication.

## Does sending my manuscript to a publisher constitute publication?

Usually, it does not. While offering to distribute copies—including the original—to a group of persons for the purpose of further distribution, public performance, or public display is a publication, sending a copy to a publisher is for the limited purpose of review. You are not authorizing the publisher to use the work, only to review it to determine if they are interested in publishing it on a basis to be determined by further negotiations.

### Does hanging my painting in an art gallery constitute publication?

No, a public display of the work does not in itself constitute publication. Under the old law, public display could constitute publication; under the new law, the original or a copy must be distributed to the public, not merely displayed.

### Is performance of a work a publication?

Generally, performance alone does not constitute publication. If, however, some form of transcription, which reduces the work to a tangible form, is being made by members of the audience with the knowledge and consent of the author, a distribution of a copy can result and the work will be published. If you are going to perform a work and you want to make absolutely certain that the performance will not constitute a publication, or be subject to compulsory licensing if it is a musical composition, you should be certain that you do not in any way consent to the making of copies or phonorecords. If someone makes an unauthorized or pirated copy, this will not result in publication of your work.

# TRANSFER OF COPYRIGHT OWNERSHIP

The following questions and answers deal with transfer of rights in copyrighted property. Attempts by nonlawyers to prepare contracts, agreements, permissions, bequests, and other legally binding instruments transferring copyright interests can be disastrous. You should definitely consult a copyright attorney before transferring any of your rights and before arranging to acquire the rights of others.

### What is the difference between an assignment and a sale?

An assignment and a sale are the same thing. Either term means that you have transferred your entire right, title, and interest in a piece of property, a right, or group of rights, usually for a specific consideration. Since copyrights are a series or group of divisible rights, you can sell or assign any or all of the rights comprising your copyright.

## What is a license?

A license is generally the grant of something less than an assignment or sale. When you grant a license, you retain title to or ownership of the work, and only limited rights are granted to the licensee for some specific use of the property. For example, you might license the performance rights for live public productions of your play while retaining all other exclusive rights.

## Is it better to assign or license a work?

One of the advantages of licensing is that the title remains with you, and you can continue to exert certain controls over the work. If anything should go wrong, you may be in a better position to deal with others while the dispute is being resolved than if you had relinquished title to the work. One disadvantage of licensing your work is that you may not be able to obtain favorable income-tax treatment. Some "assignments" are found by the Internal Revenue Service to be licenses, and some "licenses" are found to be assignments. This determination can be made for you by a tax consultant.

## Can I transfer a part of my copyright or must I transfer it in its entirety?

You may divide the rights comprising your copyright into any number of separate forms you wish. For example, you could transfer an original painting to an individual or group—retaining the right to make derivative works (such as photographic reproductions) yourself—and license another to make three-dimensional derivative works based upon the painting. You can divide not only the copyright in the work, but when the work permits, you can divide the copyright in portions of the work. For example, you can excerpt and license use of poems contained within a larger work.

## Once a transfer has been made, does the new owner have the same rights as the creator?

Yes. However, the rights transferred to the new owner may be terminated. If the author has made a grant of rights, the author or designated heirs have the right to elect to terminate the transfer at certain times specified in the Copyright Act. Termination of transfers is discussed in detail on pages 114 to 115 and 124 to 125.

### What is a nonexclusive license?

The grant of a nonexclusive license entitles the licensee to use the work, but the copyright owner can license others to make the same use of the work. For example, if you grant a nonexclusive license for the production of your book, you also could continue to publish it yourself or license others on a nonexclusive basis to publish the same book. A nonexclusive license is not a "transfer" of copyright ownership under the new Copyright Act. It is possible, therefore, to create nonexclusive licenses orally, and they will be effective between the copyright owner and the licensees. However, if there is a conflict between someone who has a nonexclusive license granted orally and someone who has a written assignment obtained in good faith, the written agreement will prevail. But if a nonexclusive license is reduced to writing and signed by the copyright owner before execution of the assignment, the nonexclusive license will prevail, even though it is not recorded in the Copyright Office. The same result occurs if the nonexclusive license is written, signed by the copyright owner, and taken by the licensee in good faith before recording of the assignment.

### What is a permission or consent-to-use license?

This is, in effect, a limited form of nonexclusive license. The main purpose of permissions or consents is to allow someone to incorporate in their own work a part of the copyrighted work of another. Thus, if you want to use a part of another's copyrighted work, and there is a question as to whether this use is permissible under the doctrine of fair use, you should obtain an express written consent or permission from the copyright owner.

### What should I be aware of if I grant such consent or permission?

If a relatively small portion of your work is being used, you may not get monetary compensation; however, as a condition for your consent to use, you can require that you be given credit for your contribution. You should insist that the publication in which your work will appear has the proper copyright notice. Also, if you are concerned about the context into which your work will be incorporated, you may wish to reserve the right to see how it will be used before granting permission. In other words, you will want to make certain that your work is not being distorted or degraded by the manner in which it is being used.

### Is it necessary to record such consent or permission with the Copyright Office?

No, they should be written, but nonexclusive licenses, such as consents or permissions to use a work, are enforceable even though they are not recorded.

### How do I obtain a consent or permission to use a portion of someone else's work?

You must contact and obtain the written permission of the copyright owner. Usually, the copyright owner will be the person or business entity named in the copyright notice. There may have been transfers of copyright ownership since publication of the copy of the work you have. Accordingly, you can arrange for a search of the Copyright Office records to determine who is the current owner of the work.

### Is a transfer of rights that is compensated by periodic royalty payments an assignment or a license?

The method of payment will not normally determine whether a transfer is an assignment or a license. Some licenses are based upon a single lump-sum payment, usually upon execution of the license agreement. Other licenses require periodic royalty payments in addition to, or in place of, a lump-sum payment. Similarly, assignments may also be based upon a single payment or a continuing royalty.

Licenses are distinguished from assignments by the nature of the ownership rights retained by the party granting the rights, not by the means of payment.

**If I transfer my work on the basis of a percentage royalty, rather than an outright payment, how do I know that it will actually be produced and distributed so that I will receive royalties?**

This is a matter of contract, not copyright, law. The contract usually will contain terms stating that the assignee or licensee must distribute a minimum number of copies for which you will receive royalties, or make a minimum royalty payment at specified time periods, or a combination of both. It is usually further provided that, upon failure to meet the conditions of the contract, the copyright will be reassigned to you or the license terminated.

**Who determines the royalty rate?**

The royalty rate is a matter of negotiation, determined by practices of the industry and individual considerations. In connection with nondramatic musical works, however, there is a compulsory royalty rate available to licensees (see Chapter 6 for full explanation of compulsory licensing). Even when nondramatic musical compositions are involved, it is possible to reach a negotiated license that differs from the compulsory license rates, although the compulsory rates have considerable effect in setting the upper limit of musical-composition royalties.

**What is required to have a valid transfer of copyright ownership such as an assignment or exclusive license?**

You must have a written document signed by the owner of the rights or an authorized agent. The transfer document need not take any special form, but it must identify the work. It is best if you can identify the work by the title, the copyright registration number, the registration date, and the author's name. Additionally, the document must specify exactly what rights are transferred. The new law makes it clear that any rights not specifically included in the agreement will not be implied to have been transferred. The document should be dated and should contain, although it is *not* an absolute requirement, a certificate of acknowledgement.

**Is it necessary to record transfers with the Copyright Office?**

Recording is not an absolute requirement for a transfer of copyright ownership to be binding, but it is necessary when conflicts with someone other than the parties arise. Accordingly, it is highly advisable in most instances. Any signed document pertaining to a copyright may be recorded with the Copyright Office upon payment of the recording fee. Recording the document, however, will likely have little effect unless the work has been registered with the Copyright Office, and the document recorded identifies the work by title and registration number.

### What is the effect of recording an assignment or other transfer of copyright ownership with the Copyright Office?

The advantage of recording with the Copyright Office is that, as a matter of law, everyone is given constructive notice of the facts stated in the document. This notice can be extremely important. You want to be certain that the person granting rights to you is authorized to do so. Additionally, you do not want that person to sell the same rights twice, placing you in a conflict with an innocent party.

### How do I avoid purchasing rights from someone who in fact does not own the rights which he purports to sell?

Before you buy, search the records of the Copyright Office. If the work is registered, the Copyright Office can inform you whether the author has transferred the work and what documents have been recorded pertaining to ownership of the copyright. There is still some danger that transfers have taken place before registration or less than two months before the transfer to you. Such transfers could create adverse rights, but a search is certainly helpful in ascertaining that the purported owner is in fact the legal owner.

### What happens to my copyright when I die? If a copyright is personal property, can it be bequeathed?

Yes, your copyright is an asset of your estate. It can be bequeathed to whomever you designate in your will. If you die intestate (without a will), it will be conveyed in accordance with the laws of intestate succession in your state.

### Does the work have to be registered with the Copyright Office in order to be bequeathed?

No, a conveyance by will or through intestate succession will occur even if the work is not registered. Since your heirs will want clear title to copyright, the executor of your estate may go through the registration process so that the probate judge can distribute the copyright in a clearly identifiable manner, that is, by reference to the copyright registration number.

### Should the Copyright Office be notified of a transfer upon death of the copyright owner?

Yes. If the work is registered, a certified copy of the decree of distribution of the estate, showing the new owner or owners, the registration number, the title of the work, the author, and the registration date should be recorded with the Copyright Office. If the work is unregistered, it is advisable for the executor to register the work before the assets of the estate are distributed. Once registered, the decree of distribution identifying the work, and the heir or legatee receiving the same, can be recorded. Your heirs will be unable to bring a suit for copyright infringement without both registration of the work and a record of the transfer to them.

### Should the Copyright Office be notified upon death of an author?

Since the duration of the copyright will be determined for many works by the author's life span, the Copyright Office keeps separate records relating to the death of authors. If you own a work created by another and the author dies, you can record a statement of the date of death of the author. Your identity and your interest in the work and the source of your information as to the author's death must be contained in the statement. You can also record a statement that the author is still living to indicate that the work still has more than fifty years before expiration.

## JOINT OWNERSHIP

This section pertains to works created and/or owned by two or more parties. It often comes as a surprise to authors, but unless there is an agreement to the contrary, any one of several joint owners can unilaterally grant nonexclusive licenses and make use of a joint work that cannot be controlled by the remaining owners. Joint owners should be aware of their respective rights so that they can supplement them by contract if they wish to make special conditions and agreements among themselves.

## I have written a book with another person. Do we each register a separate copyright for our respective interests or do we have one, undivided copyright?

If the contributions of each author are merged into an inseparable work or interdependent parts of a unitary whole, the authors will be joint authors and co-owners of a single copyright. Only one claim to copyright should be registered. If one "author" is merely supplementing the authorship of the other—for example, if someone is commissioned to illustrate a text—the creator of the supplementary material is not an author of the overall work. The author of the main body of the work will be the sole author. If the book is a collective work with separable parts, the authors of individual contributions will each have their own copyrights, which are independent of the copyright for the collective work.

## Does each owner of a joint work have an equal interest in the property?

The authors of a joint work are co-owners of the copyright. The rights are not partitioned or divided; rather, each author owns an undivided interest in the work. Their interests will be equal, and they will extend to all of the rights comprising the copyright. Thus, three joint authors will have undivided one-third interests.

## Can joint authors agree that one author shall have a larger interest in the copyright than the remaining authors?

Although it will be presumed, in the absence of a formal agreement between the co-owners, that their interests are equal, the joint authors can agree among themselves that their ownership interests shall be divided in any manner they wish. If the shares are not equal, the unequal division should be reflected in a written document recorded with the Copyright Office.

## Does the fact that one person did more to reduce the work to tangible form—for example, by a larger contribution to the writing—entitle that person to a greater share of copyright ownership in a joint work?

The parties can agree in advance that it does, but unless there is such an agreement, the quantity of the contribution will not determine the share of ownership of copyright. Moreover, the fact that a person puts the work into tangible form does not necessarily mean that person made the greater contribution. For example, a ghostwriter may not contribute as much creativity as the "resource" person, who does not actually write, but whose knowledge or expertise may form the foundation of the work.

## Can a ghostwriter be a copyright owner?

The ghostwriter, or other facilitator, may or may not be a joint author and co-owner of the resulting work. A ghostwriter may simply be employed or hired for a stipulated wage, fee, or other compensation. Under such an agreement, the ghostwriter will be preparing the work within the scope of his or her employment, and the employer will legally be the author of a work made "for hire." If the employer and the ghostwriter agree that their efforts are to be merged in one unitary whole, with neither party employing the other, the result will be a joint work that is co-owned. It is extremely advantageous to reach a written understanding as to ownership of the product before a joint effort is undertaken.

## Can any one owner unilaterally assign or license rights in a joint work?

Yes, it must be realized that any joint owner—regardless of how small his or her interest in the copyright may be—can reproduce, distribute, adapt, display, or perform the work without the consent of the other owners. In addition, as long as it does not destroy the work, each joint owner can license his or her rights without the permission of the others. However, any license will be necessarily nonexclusive, since the remaining joint owners can also grant nonexclusive licenses. Any owner who grants a license will have a duty to account to the remaining joint owners for each of their shares of the proceeds received from the license.

## How can such unilateral actions be prevented?

It is best to have an agreement among the co-owners stating that no one owner will sell, license, transfer, or convey any part of, or rights in, the work, or unilaterally use the work without the consent of all, or a specified percentage, of the co-owners. In the agreement, you should identify the work by copyright registration number, date, title, and authors' names. Then, you should record the agreement with the Copyright Office. If you are the purchaser of a work which is controlled by joint owners, you should contact each of the current co-owners.

### Can one co-owner buy out another's interest?

Yes.

### If a copyrighted joint work is licensed, for example, to a publisher, will the license be invalidated if I sell my joint ownership interest to someone who is neither the publisher nor a co-owner?

No, unless the contract with the publisher or other joint owners expressly prohibits this. Usually, licensing arrangements will involve only the payment of money to the co-owners, and the publisher will not be concerned as to whether the money is paid to you or your transferee. The right to receive royalties will normally be transferable without the publisher's consent.

### What happens if one co-owner dies? Will the remaining owners now have title to the deceased owner's interest in the work?

No, this is part of the deceased owner's personal estate and will descend to his or her heirs. Although not common, the co-owners can enter into an agreement in which they have the right to buy an owner's interest upon his or her death, or they can create, by assignment, a joint property right in which the copyright automatically passes to the surviving owners upon an owner's death.

## COLLECTIVE WORK

Collective works are comprised of several separate, independent works. Both the independent works and the collection may be copyrighted and registered separately. Anthologies, encyclopedias, and periodicals are examples of collective works. The author of a contribution to a collective work should be aware of his or her rights and of those of the author of the collection.

### If I contribute an article to a collective work, such as a magazine, have I automatically assigned my rights to the magazine publisher, and if so, can I get them back?

The ownership of the copyright in a contribution to a collective work resides initially in the author. Unless the author expressly transfers copyright ownership in the contribution to the owner of the collective work, the owner of the collective work is presumed to have acquired only the right to reproduce and distribute the contribution as part of the collective work, revisions of the collective work, or later collective works in the "same series." Since transfers of copyright ownership must be in writing in order to take effect, express oral statements would not transfer ownership from the author of the contribution to the author of the collective work.

### If I contribute an article to a collective work, should my name appear on the copyright notice and/or registration?

Unless you have assigned the copyright to the owner of the collective work, your name should appear in a separate copyright notice associated with your contribution, and you should separately register your work. It is not absolutely necessary for copyright protection that your name appear in a separate copyright notice since the blanket notice at the front of the collective work will protect your contribution (unless it is an advertisement). However, failure to place your own notice on your contribution may give the impression that the copyright owner of the collective work owns your work.

### If the collective work is registered in the publisher's name, can I also register my contribution?

Yes, and you should.

### I am planning to publish a collection of stories from different authors, some of which are copyrighted (which I have permission to use) and some of which are in the public domain. Can I copyright this work in my name, even though I have not added any new material?

Yes, you may copyright the collection in your name. Since there is creativity and authorship in compiling, collecting, organizing, and selecting, you have created a copyrightable work. You should remember, however, that although no one else can reproduce and distribute your copyrighted collection, others are free to use the works in the public domain and the same copyrighted materials if they can obtain permission from the original copyright owners. Later authors may be able to use the same individual components alone or in new collections that include some of the same works you have used.

# DERIVATIVE WORKS

This section relates to new works based on a preexisting work that has been transformed, recast, or adapted into another form, such as a translation, dramatization, musical arrangement, editorial revision, annotation, or condensation. The modification or adaptation must contain some creative authorship or originality; it cannot, for example, merely be comprised of stenographic changes.

### Does the term "derivative works" apply only to the situation in which the author of the adapted work is different from the author of the underlying work?

No, the author of the original work and the derivative work may or may not be the same. For example, you may adapt your novel to produce a drama. The drama is derivative work, regardless of who prepares the adaptation.

### Can I make a derivative work based upon the copyrighted work of another author?

Not unless you obtain permission from the copyright owner of the basic work. One of the exclusive rights of a copyright owner is the right to prohibit others from making derivative works. If you adapt another's work without his consent, you will be a copyright infringer and subject to the penalties for such unauthorized use.

### If I want to make a derivative work based upon someone else's work, such as a dramatization of a novel, what is the procedure for obtaining permission?

You must contact the copyright owner for his or her consent. You may have to pay for such a consent or license. Whether or not the copyright owner will be willing to grant permission to adapt the work will depend on a number of factors, such as how you intend to use the existing material, the compensation the original author will receive, your past experience, and your reputation.

### If I am the author of a derivative work based upon the original work of another person—for example, if I make a translation—will I own the copyright in the derivative work or will the creator of the underlying work own the copyright?

You are the author of the derivative work and accordingly will own the copyright. It is entirely possible, however, that the owner of the underlying work will require that you assign the derivative work to him or her as an express condition to the grant of permission. In such an event you might receive a royalty and be acknowledged on the work and in the Copyright Office as the author, but not own the copyright in the work.

### If I obtain a compulsory license to use a musical composition am I entitled to make a derivative work based upon the musical composition?

No, you are entitled to make a new musical arrangement, but the new arrangement cannot change the basic melody or fundamental character of the work. You must obtain the express consent of the copyright owner to make derivative works if you want to adapt the work beyond the limited changes allowed under the compulsory-license provisions.

### Does a derivative work require a separate copyright registration? If, for example, I make an abridgment of my original work, do I need to register this abridgment in order to have the full advantages of registration?

Yes, a derivative work is copyrightable and has a life of its own, beginning at the time of its creation. The copyright notice should bear the year the derivative work was first published, although the year of first publication of the underlying work can also be shown in the notice.

**If I allow another person to use my work in order to create a derivative work, would I be entitled to any share in the profits?**

In order for someone to prepare a derivative work based upon your work, he or she must obtain your consent, and you can negotiate whatever terms you wish for such use, including monetary compensation in the form of royalties.

**When I grant permission to someone to make a derivative work, am I barred from making the same use of my work?**

Not necessarily, but as a practical matter it is likely that you will be. This determination can be the subject of license negotiations for creation of the derivative work. For many works, you would agree not to create derivative works yourself or to grant the same right to others.

# WORKS FOR HIRE

A work made "for hire" is prepared by an employee within the scope of his or her employment. This was true under the old law as well as the new Copyright Act. The new law further provides that many types of specifically ordered or commissioned works are works made "for hire," *if* the parties agree *in writing* that the work shall be considered a work made for hire. This requirement of a written agreement favors the actual creator of the work. The need for a written agreement, in situations that cannot be characterized as employer–employee relationships, will undoubtedly come as an unpleasant surprise to those who in the past have contracted orally with authors for the creation of copyrightable works. Illustrators, translators, adaptors, and ghostwriters who sell their works as independent contractors will retain the copyright in these works unless there is a writing specifically commissioning the work. This is true even though the parties may believe that the copyright was transferred with the original of the work.

In a "for hire" situation the *employer* is legally considered the "author" and owner of the copyright.

## Is any work I create in connection with my job the property of my employer?

Generally, yes, if creation of the work was within the scope of your duties as an employee. You cannot decide to keep for yourself "special" ideas or decide to set aside, to develop "on your own time," projects arising from your employment. If you wish to reserve certain rights to your creative works, you should specifically do so in an employment contract with your employer.

## Does my employer have any rights to creative works that I produce when I am away from the job premises?

Yes, if the work produced is within the scope of your employment. The reason is that creativity cannot be regulated in the same way as other types of work. Breakthroughs, solutions to problems, and creative insights may come at any time, not necessarily during office hours. Such productivity will be deemed to be part of the terms of your employment if the subject matter is within the scope of your employment.

## What if the type of work is completely unrelated to my job?

If the creative work produced at home was clearly unrelated to your employment, it would not be made "for hire." For example, if you are a commercial artist hired to do fashion layouts, but away from the job you produce fine-art paintings entirely different in nature from the commercial art, the fine art would be your property.

## Would it ever be possible for me to gain ownership of my "for hire" work?

Yes, the rights could be assigned to you. If the company or person for whom you prepared the "for hire" work wanted it for a single purpose or short-term use, they may be willing to transfer the rights to you.

## Can a "for hire" work be created for someone other than an employer?

Yes, a commissioned work *may* be made "for hire." If the work falls in any of the following categories it may be a work "for hire": a contribution to a collective work, a part of a motion picture or other audiovisual work, a translation, a supplementary work (a work for use with a basic work by another author), a compilation, an instructional text, test-answer material, or an atlas. In order for a commissioned work to be made "for hire," it *must* be expressly agreed in writing by you that the work is made on a "for hire" basis.

# DESIGN PATENTS AND COPYRIGHTS

Some creative works can be the subject of both design patent and copyright protection. Other works can be protected only by a design patent or only by copyright. The requirements for and the protection afforded by the design patent and copyright laws differ, and the following questions and answers explore these differences.

### What is a design patent?

Design patents protect ornamental designs of manufactured articles. To qualify for a design patent, the ornamental design must be new and unobvious. A design patent entitles the owner to prohibit others from making, using, or selling a product including the design. It is the overall aesthetic appearance of the product that is protected, not the product itself or any mechanical or utilitarian feature of the product. Mechanical or utilitarian features can be protected by utility patents, if they amount to inventions, but they are not protectable under the design-patent law. A design patent has a maximum life of fourteen years, after which the patent rights expire.

### What types of articles are protected by design patents?

Examples of manufactured articles incorporating ornamental designs that are frequently the subject of design patents are dolls, furniture, bottles and containers, jewelry, vehicles, boats, appliances, game boards, type fonts, and sporting equipment. Virtually any article having an appearance that is not totally dictated or determined by functional or utilitarian considerations can be the subject of a design patent.

### What similar types of articles are protected by copyright?

Three-dimensional works of fine and applied art, as well as works of artistic craftsmanship, can be the subject of copyright.

Thus, artistic craftsmanship incorporated into useful articles can be copyrighted, if pictorial, graphic, or sculptural works recognizable apart from the article itself are included in the useful article. Mechanical or utilitarian aspects of articles are not copyrightable. Thus, statuary, carvings, jewelry, dolls, and other useful articles that are embossed, painted, molded, etched, or whatever with designs are examples of copyrightable three-dimensional articles.

### Is it harder to obtain a design patent than a copyright?

Yes, copyright requires some small quantity of originality, but design patents require not only originality, but invention. A design must be unobvious to those skilled in the particular field of endeavor in order for the design to constitute a patentable invention.

### What is an example of an article that can be the subject of both a copyright and a design patent?

A piece of jewelry can be protected under both copyright and design-patent laws. Dolls and game boards are other examples.

### When is an article protectable under the design-patent laws but not under the copyright laws?

An example might be a new and inventive bottle design. If the bottle is smooth and unsculptured and yet has proportions and a shape that are novel and unobvious, it could be the subject of a design patent. The same bottle, however, is not copyrightable under the new Copyright Act, since it is a useful article that does not contain pictorial, graphic, or sculptural work that could be separately recognized from the bottle.

### What would be required for a useful article, such as a bottle, to be copyrightable?

If the bottle had a rose embossed into the side or a tree etched on the surface, it would contain copyrightable subject matter that could be recognized apart from the bottle. Such a bottle could be the subject of both design-patent and copyright protection. There currently are proposals before Congress that would make the shape of such a bottle copyrightable, but under the Copyright Act of

1976, the mere shape, as opposed to the rose design, of a utilitarian article is not copyrightable.

### How complex and costly is the procedure for obtaining a design patent?

It is significantly more difficult, costly, and time consuming to obtain a design patent than it is to register a claim to copyright. While theoretically a person may prepare and file his or her own design-patent application, it is more difficult than a copyright application, and usually patent counsel is required. In addition to the problems connected with preparation and filing of the design-patent application, the applicant normally will have to submit legal arguments to the Patent and Trademark Office relating to the standard of invention. For some products, however, such as game boards or jewelry, the additional cost of obtaining a design patent is justified, and for utilitarian articles having a pleasing shape but no independently recognizable design, it may be the only form of protection available.

### How does design-patent protection differ from copyright protection?

One major difference is that a design patent will afford protection against an infringer who reinvents or re-creates the design without ever having seen the patent or patented article. Copyright infringement, by contrast, requires access to the copyright owner's work and use or copying of the work. Independent creation of a product can be design-patent infringement but cannot be copyright infringement.

### When do I have to file for a design patent?

A design-patent application must be filed in the United States Patent and Trademark Office within one year of the first public use, offer for sale, or disclosure of the invention in a printed publication. If the application is not filed before that one-year period expires, the design-patent rights will fall into the public domain. If foreign patent rights are significant, you should file the design-patent application in the United States *before* any public use, offer for sale, or description in a printed publication.

### If I have failed to file a design-patent application in a timely manner, are all of my rights lost?

No, only your design-patent rights are lost. If the article can be the subject of copyright protection, your copyright will remain unaffected by loss of your design-patent rights. If you have published the work without a copyright notice, however, you will only have five years in which to discover and correct that defect (see section on copyright notice).

## PUBLIC DOMAIN

These questions and answers focus on the permissible use of materials in the public domain. Public domain refers to materials that all members of the public can freely copy, distribute, or otherwise use without restriction or need of a license from another party. Public-domain materials include published uncopyrighted works, works in which the copyright has expired, and works that inherently are not copyrightable or protected under other laws. Use of these materials is permissible, but it is often difficult to determine whether or not a given work has fallen into the public domain.

### Can I use a work in the public domain without any further procedure—investigation, notification, or request for permission to use?

Yes, if it really is in the public domain. In view of the difficulty of determining whether or not a work is in the public domain, you should consult a copyright attorney if you intend to use material believed to be in the public domain.

### If I use public domain material, does that prevent me from obtaining my own copyright on the work in which I have incorporated the material?

No, you will have a copyright in your contribution to the resulting work, but you cannot copyright the public-domain portion.

### Can I reproduce in its entirety a work in the public domain, and distribute and market it for profit?

Yes, if it is in the public domain; so can any other party.

## Can I copyright such a work?

No, you cannot copyright a public-domain work that has merely been reproduced. Moreover, a copyright is created for the benefit of and is owned by the author of a work. You cannot claim authorship in the work of another merely by reproducing it.

## Once a work is in the public domain, can the originator of the work reinstate the copyright?

No, once a work falls into the public domain it will irretrievably remain available.

## If a work does not carry a copyright notice, does that mean it is in the public domain?

Generally, works published without copyright notice are in the public domain. However, the absence of copyright notice does not necessarily mean the work is in the public domain. Under the Copyright Act of 1976, failure to place the proper copyright notice on a published work can be corrected. If the error is corrected within five years of publication, the work will not fall into the public domain. Additionally, unpublished works do not require a copyright notice to be entitled to full copyright protection.

## How can I investigate whether or not a work without a copyright notice is actually in the public domain, or if it is still the property of the originator who might correct the notice and enforce the copyright at a later time?

First, determine whether the work is published. Unpublished works do not require a notice. Second, if the work was published, determine when the work was first published and, if possible, when your copy was published. Works published with the copyright owner's consent without the proper copyright notice before 1978 will be in the public domain. For works published after 1977, the ability to correct omission of the copyright notice is lost after five years from publication. Third, determine whether the work is based upon another underlying work that is copyrighted. Fourth, take this information to your attorney.

## Will the Copyright Office tell me if a particular work is in the public domain?

No, the Copyright Office will provide information as to whether a claim to copyright is registered, if you can properly identify the work (by title, author, and, if available, copyright owner). Legal opinions as to whether or not a work is in the public domain are not supplied.

## Is a work that has not been copyrighted in the United States but has a foreign copyright in the public domain in the United States?

No, the United States is a signatory to several international copyright conventions and treaties, and a work carrying the correct international copyright notice is protected in the United States.

## Since United States government publications are not copyrighted, are they in the public domain and can I use these materials?

Yes, works prepared by United States government employees as part of their official duties are not copyrightable, and you are free to use these works. However, works prepared by state and municipal government employees are not governed by the rule and can be copyrighted.

## Do I have to identify the source of materials emanating from the United States government?

Yes, if your work consists preponderantly of a United States government work or works. You must place a notice on your work identifying either your copyrightable portion or the part of the work extracted from United States government publications.

# FAIR USE

This section deals with permissible or "fair use" of the copyrighted works of others. If you intend to use another's copyrighted material, you should do so with great caution since there is a thin line between fair use and infringement. If you have any doubts about using such material, you should obtain permission from the copyright owner and/or seek advice from a copyright attorney.

### Do "public domain" and "fair use" mean the same thing?

No, "public domain" refers to the vast body of works that are not copyrighted and that anyone can use without restriction. "Fair use" refers to a limited use of a copyrighted work for certain purposes without the copyright owner's permission.

### What factors determine whether a use of a copyrighted work is a fair use?

Four main factors are considered: (1) the purpose and character of the use, including whether such use is of a commercial nature or is for nonprofit educational purposes; (2) the nature of the copyrighted work; (3) the amount of material used in relation to the copyrighted work as a whole; (4) the effect of the use upon the potential market for, or value of, the copyrighted work. While other factors can be considered, one or more of the above will often predominate in determining fair use.

### How does the purpose for which the material is used affect the ability to make fair use of a work?

The Copyright Act includes a list of purposes that have, in previous litigation, been found to be permissible reasons or motives for use of another's copyrighted work. The list of acceptable purposes includes criticism, comment, news reporting, teaching (including multiple copies for classroom use), scholarship, or research. While commercial or for-profit purposes are permitted also, they tend to weigh against fair use. A "proper" purpose, however, is only one consideration and will not alone justify use. The following other factors must be considered also in determining whether there has been a fair use.

### Does the nature of the work affect fair use?

Theoretically, at least, all works are subject to fair use, but the nature of the work will make a difference as to the type of use permitted. For example, a black-and-white photographic reproduction of a large piece of statuary used by an art critic might well be considered fair use; a color, life-size, photographic reproduction of a painting used by the same critic might not. The large color photograph might be considered derivative work, which goes beyond fair use and requires the consent of the copyright owner.

### How much of a work can be used and still qualify as a fair use?

There is no absolute answer—such as a certain number of words—but, as a general rule, the smaller the use the more likely it is to be fair. "Small" and "large" are determined by comparison to the original work as a whole. For example, fifty words taken from an encyclopedia may be a fair use; however, fifty words extracted from a short essay may be a copyright infringement, since a substantial portion of the total work was used.

### How important is the effect of the use on the potential market of the original work?

The most common determining factor in the courts for judging fair use is whether the use has an adverse economic impact upon the copyrighted work. Thus, if the asserted fair use directly competes with the original work, it is likely to be found to be a copyright infringement, not a fair use.

### What if my use gives economic benefits to the original work, such as publicizing it? Will I have greater latitude in the amount I can use?

The fact that your use enhances the potential market or value of the copyrighted work will not be given great weight. You cannot justify wholesale use of another's work on these grounds.

### When making a fair use of copyrighted material, must I cite the copied work or give credit to the original author in any way?

No, this is not required under the fair-use doctrine. However, failure to give credit to the original author may raise questions about your motives—a factor to be considered when determining whether fair use may be claimed. You may help resolve doubts by crediting the author in footnotes, or in your text, and, if your use is a fair one, you do not need permission to cite the author's name and work.

**Is it necessary to obtain permission from the author to list the title of the work in the bibliography of my book and to include a short description of the work?**

No, a title cannot be copyrighted, and if the description is in your own words, it is a type of derivative work that is a fair use and does not require permission.

**If I review or critique another's work, must I have the permission of the person whose work I am reviewing?**

Not unless you quote at length from the work reviewed. You will be primarily creating your own work. Criticism is not derivative of the work reviewed, and fair use does not apply if you are expressing your own opinion in your own words. To the extent that you are quoting from the other person's work, you are limited to fair use. In connection with criticism and review, however, you generally will have greater latitude in the amount of material that can be used under the fair-use doctrine.

# INFRINGEMENT

This section on infringement gives only a brief overview in order to make you aware of your rights and recourse should anyone violate your copyright. If you discover an infringement and cannot convince the offending party to stop, you should hire a copyright attorney promptly before further harm occurs.

**What constitutes copyright infringement?**

Copyright infringement occurs whenever someone exercises any one of the exclusive rights comprising your copyright without your permission—unless the act constitutes fair use or some other specific statutory exception to your exclusive rights. Thus, if someone who is not authorized to do so reproduces, distributes, adapts, displays, or performs your copyrighted work, you should carefully investigate the unauthorized use and determine whether it is an infringement or falls within a statutory exception to your exclusive rights.

## If I discover someone is using my copyrighted work without my consent, what recourse do I have?

If any of your exclusive rights are violated, you are entitled to file a lawsuit in a Federal District Court seeking an order to stop the infringement as well as damages and profits. However, if you have conveyed certain rights under a contract and you believe the conditions of the contract are being violated, this type of problem may be a matter of contract law, not copyright infringement. Contract disputes will normally be litigated in a state court.

## What types of remedies or compensation can I obtain in an infringement action against the party using my work?

Any or all of the following remedies may be mandated by a judge in an infringement action:

1. An injunction preventing the infringer from further use of your work
2. Impounding and destruction of the infringing materials and the articles by which they are reproduced
3. Compensation to you in the form of recovery of your actual damages and the infringer's additional profits, if any, obtained as a result of using your work
4. If your work was registered before the infringement began, you can also elect to obtain statutory damages, which are particularly important when you cannot prove actual damages
5. If your work was registered before the infringement began, you may also be able to recover your attorney fees
6. Recovery of the costs of litigation

Statutory damages will range between $250 and $10,000 unless the infringement is willful, in which case you can recover up to $50,000.

## Can I bring an infringement action if I have not registered my work with the Copyright Office?

The work must be registered with the Copyright Office in order to obtain any of the legal remedies for infringement. It is possible, but not advisable, to *begin* the infringement action before the application for copyright registration is filed. Registration before the infringement acts begin—or in the case of a published work, within three months of publication—is necessary in order to recover statutory damages and attorney fees.

### What should I do first when I discover that my work is being used without my consent?

It is best to give notice to the person who you *believe* is an infringer stating that he or she appears to be violating your copyright. You may be able to reconcile the situation amicably and avoid the considerable expense of litigation. This person could be unaware that he or she has committed an infringing act, and may be willing to terminate use of your work and/or compensate you for any loss; or, the fault may be yours. You may have placed copies outside of your control without proper notice, and the other person may be an innocent infringer, simply using materials that he or she believed were not copyrighted.

### If I give notice to the infringer, but the infringement continues what should I do next?

If you have not already done so, see a copyright attorney.

### Would the fact that the infringer is an innocent infringer reduce the amount of compensation?

This is quite likely, especially when you have contributed to the infringement by allowing the work to be published without the proper copyright notice. In fact, you will be barred from the recovery of actual and statutory damages, and the court may decide that you should receive no compensation at all. You will not, however, be barred from obtaining an injunction, unless your work has fallen into the public domain or unless the court should decide to create a compulsory license because of the innocent nature of the infringement.

# ROYALTIES, COMPULSORY LICENSING, AND THE COPYRIGHT ROYALTY TRIBUNAL

### What is a royalty?

A royalty is a form of compensation paid for a license or assignment of one or more of the exclusive rights in a copyrighted work.

It usually consists of periodic payments based upon a percentage (the royalty rate) of the sales of copies or performances of the work, but a royalty can be paid in one lump sum.

### To what types of work do royalties apply?

Any copyrighted work or any exclusive right in a copyrighted work can be licensed or transferred for a royalty.

### How are royalty rates established?

Generally, a royalty rate is fixed by negotiation between the parties to a license or transfer agreement, and is largely influenced by a range of royalty rates common to particular industries. In order to avoid the devaluing effect of inflation, it is preferable for royalties to be set on a percentage basis. However, in some cases, royalties may be established as a fixed-dollar amount per unit or copy of the work sold.

### What is compulsory licensing?

There are two types of licenses—consentual and compulsory. Consentual licenses are negotiated between the parties to the license agreement. Either party can refuse to enter into the license agreement, and the copyright owner can refuse to grant a license in the work if the desired conditions are not met. Under compulsory license, however, the copyright owner is compelled to grant a license if certain terms set by the Copyright Act—modified from time to time by the Copyright Royalty Tribunal—are met. Although the terms of the license may be negotiated, if this is agreeable to both parties, the copyright owner cannot refuse to grant certain rights if the other party qualifies for and insists on a compulsory license.

### Does that mean that anyone can use my work, even without my permission, under compulsory license?

Yes, if the minimum conditions of compulsory licensing are present; otherwise, the copyright owner may refuse to license the work and retain all of the exclusive rights.

## What types of work are subject to compulsory licensing?

The primary areas subject to compulsory licensing under the Copyright Act are:

1. Nondramatic musical works after phonorecords of the work have been distributed publicly under the authority of the copyright owner

2. Secondary transmissions by cable systems (cable television) of a primary transmission embodying the performance or display of a work

3. Public performances through coin-operated phonorecord players (jukeboxes)

4. Noncommercial broadcasting of certain previously published works if the copyright owners and noncommercial broadcasters cannot reach a negotiated agreement

5. In some situations, as determined by a court, when an innocent infringer begins use of a work due to the omission of the copyright notice

## What is the Copyright Royalty Tribunal?

It is an administrative body whose function is to:

1. Adjust, as it may deem necessary, the royalty rates for compulsory licensing of nondramatic musical works

2. Adjust, as required, the royalty rate for compulsory licenses for jukeboxes

3. Establish and adjust rates for cable television and noncommercial-broadcasting compulsory licenses

4. Collect and distribute royalty fees to copyright owners who make a claim for compensation for the public performance of their works on jukeboxes

5. Collect and distribute royalties to copyright owners who make a claim for compensation for performance and display of their works by transmission through cable television.

## In regard to nondramatic musical works, how may others use my work under a compulsory license?

Once you have recorded your musical composition *and* distributed copies to the public, others may make their own recordings of your nondramatic musical composition for public distribution. Anyone wishing to obtain a compulsory license to use your work must also notify you and pay the compulsory license royalty rate. The compulsory license granted, however, is only for the recording and distribution of phonorecords to the public and does *not* include the right to publicly perform the work—that requires a consentual license from you. Performing rights societies, such as the American Society of Composers, Authors, and Publishers (ASCAP) or Broadcast Music, Inc. (BMI) will monitor clubs, theaters, or wherever musical works are publicly performed, and will extract royalties which are paid to the copyright owners on a formula basis (see page 182).

### Does compulsory license entitle others to make an exact copy of my sound recording?

No, compulsory licensing does not extend to the duplication of the sound recordings of the musical work. The licensee may use only the underlying musical composition and lyrics to make his or her own recordings with hired artists. A compulsory licensee can create a different arrangement of the work as long as the fundamental character of the work is not changed. It is not permissible to obtain copyright protection in any changes in the arrangement unless the copyright owner consents.

### Will I receive any compensation for this use of my work?

Yes, if you have registered a claim to copyright in your work with the Copyright Office. Anyone obtaining a compulsory license must notify you of the intention to use your work within thirty days before or after public distribution of phonorecords. You then are entitled to collect royalties for each phonorecord distributed. If you do not receive timely payment of the requisite royalty, you may terminate the compulsory license.

### What is the royalty rate for use of my nondramatic musical work?

For each nondramatic musical work embodied in a phonorecord, the compulsory license royalty rate is the larger of (1) 2¾ cents per composition; or (2) ½ cent per minute of playing time or fraction thereof.

## Are there any provisions regarding when payment of the royalty shall be made?

Royalty payments shall be made on or before the twentieth day of each month and shall include all royalties for the preceding month.

## Will anything prevent my nondramatic musical work from being subject to a compulsory license?

If you do not make and publicly distribute phonorecords of your work, it cannot become subject to a compulsory license.

## If my work is not registered, will this prevent others from using it under a compulsory license?

No, it will only prohibit the receipt of royalties. If your work is not registered and/or your ownership of the work cannot be located in the Copyright Office records, the person wishing to obtain a compulsory license must simply notify the Copyright Office of intent to use the work—no royalty payments need be made by the compulsory licensee for unregistered works.

## Does compulsory licensing apply to use of nondramatic musical work in theaters, bars, radio, and so on?

No, this use of your work constitutes a public performance, which requires consentual licensing. Only the making and distribution of phonorecords to the public for *private* use is subject to compulsory licensing.

## How can I collect royalties for my musical work that is publicly performed in theaters, bars, radio?

You can exercise your rights as a copyright owner to control the public performance of your work and arrange for those using your work to make royalty payments. If your work is publicly performed without your consent, this is copyright infringement. Most owners of copyrighted nondramatic musical works belong to a performing rights society, such as ASCAP or BMI. These societies negotiate licenses for public performance, collect and distribute royalties to the artist, and monitor the industry for infringement or other violations of artists' rights.

**If my work is played on a jukebox, how am I compensated?**

In this case, the Copyright Royalty Tribunal—not the individual copyright owner—initially collects royalty fees from jukebox operators and distributes the royalties to the copyright owners. There is a compulsory licensing fee of $8 per year per jukebox.

**How do I claim royalties from jukebox licenses?**

If you believe that your work has been played publicly on jukeboxes, you should make a claim to the Copyright Royalty Tribunal each year during the month of January. Usually, this is done by the organization representing the artist, but if you are not affiliated with a performing rights society, you may make the claim yourself. Write to the Copyright Royalty Tribunal, 1111 20th Street N.W., Washington, D.C. 20036, for information about procedure.

**How am I compensated for performance or display of my work when it is transmitted on cable television?**

When you negotiate for the performance or display of your work by a primary television broadcaster, the resulting license will be consentual, not compulsory. However, the primary broadcaster's signal may be picked up by a cable system and retransmitted to a larger audience. Such retransmissions are subject to compulsory licensing. This licensing applies to retransmission of both distant and near signals—only distant signals which are retransmitted give rise to royalties to the copyright owner.

**How do I receive the cable TV compulsory-licensing royalties?**

The compulsory-licensing fees for cable-system transmissions are collected by the Copyright Royalty Tribunal and distributed to the copyright owners who make a written claim each year during the month of July. If you have such a work, write to the Copyright Royalty Tribunal for information on how to file a claim.

# 6 special copyright situations

## LIBRARIES AND ARCHIVES: REPRODUCTION AND DISTRIBUTION OF COPYRIGHTED WORKS

The library photocopying machine—whether in the back room and operated by library personnel, or out front and operated by library users—is a potential fountainhead of copyright infringement. It is not surprising, therefore, that among the more significant "sticking points" causing delay in the enactment of the new copyright law was Section 108, granting an exception to copyright infringement for libraries and archives.

Every library and archive in the United States should have at least one copy of *Copyright Office Circular R21* entitled, "Reproduction of Copyrighted Works by Educators and Librarians." Libraries and archives should establish a firm policy with regard to photocopying (and other types of reproductions, such as taping) based upon study of the new copyright law and related regulations. *Circular R21* is an excellent source for the materials needed to develop such a policy. The relevant statute, regulations, debate in Congress, and guidelines of the National Commission on New

Technological Uses of Copyrighted Works are collected and set forth in a reasonably well-structured manner.

While not a substitute for a thorough examination of the statute, regulations, and legislative history, the following overview of the limited exemption from copyright infringement granted to libraries and archives should be helpful in understanding the scope and purposes of Section 108 of the Copyright Act.

## Statutory Basis for Exemption

The section dealing with library reproduction and distribution of copyrighted material is intended for the benefit of the *library* and its employees, not for the benefit of library *users*. The general public is *not* given an exemption from copyright infringement simply because the copying or arranging for copying is done in a library. The library may be exempt if specified conditions are met, but the library user may nevertheless be a copyright infringer. The library's exemption cannot be claimed by the library user.

The copyright owner has the exclusive right to reproduce or copy his or her work and to distribute copies to the public. Accordingly, either copying or distributing copies of a work can be an infringement of copyright, unless a limitation modifies these rights. Section 108 of the Copyright Act is a "limitation" on the exclusive rights granted to the owner of copyright under Section 106. This limitation is an outgrowth of the old, judge-made law that has attempted to apply the doctrine of "fair use" to library and archive situations, but it clearly goes beyond fair use. The more general fair-use limitation on a copyright owner's exclusive rights has also been codified in the new law in Section 107. Thus, the Copyright Act sets forth a statutory scheme that can be summarized as follows:

1. The copyright owner has the exclusive right to make and distribute reproductions of a work, unless otherwise limited (Section 106).

2. Anyone, including libraries, archives, and library users, may make a "fair use" of a copyrighted work for certain purposes, and under specified conditions, without infringing the copyright owner's exclusive rights (Section 107).

3. Libraries and archives can reproduce and distribute copies and phonorecords, even though such reproduction and/or distribution would have gone beyond fair use, *if* the reproduction and distribution meet the conditions of Section 108.

What can a library or archive copy and distribute without fear of copyright infringement? The answer has three major components. First, any work in the public domain can be copied by libraries, or anyone for that matter. The problem is to be certain of what is or is not in the public domain. Second, libraries, as well as others, can make and distribute copies constituting a fair use of copyrighted material. However, the line between fair use and unfair use is not always clear. Third, libraries may reproduce and distribute copies in accordance with Section 108 of the Copyright Act, without determining whether or not the material is in the public domain or the copying constitutes fair use.

## Threshold Conditions Applicable to All Reproductions and Distributions

There are five basic or "threshold" conditions, all of which must always be met, to qualify a library for exemption from copyright infringement under Section 108: (1) the library must be open to the public; (2) the copy cannot be made for profit; (3) the notice of copyright must appear on the copy; (4) no more than one copy may be made; (5) making the copy cannot violate an agreement.

***Library must be open to the public.*** The definition of a "library" or "archives" is not specified in the copyright law. However, Section 108 states that in addition to public libraries, a collection of works will also qualify as a library open to the public if it is "available not only to researchers affiliated with the library or archives or with the institution of which it is a part, but also to other persons doing research in a specialized field." Accordingly, in addition to municipal libraries and libraries at educational institutions, libraries maintained by business or commercial entities—and even by individuals—can qualify for a Section 108 exemption.

**Copy cannot be made for profit.** The requirement that the copy be "made without any purpose of direct or indirect advantage" has raised questions as to whether a copy made by a library of a profit-making business will always be made for profit, or, in the statutory language, for the "purpose of direct or *indirect* commercial advantage." The legislative history of Section 108, however, makes it clear that the library of a for-profit company qualifies as a library entitled to make Section 108 reproductions and distributions, even though it is indirectly going to realize a "commercial advantage." The key or determinative factor is whether or not the specific reproduction or distribution of the copy or phonorecord was done for the purpose of commercial advantage. There must be "commercial advantage" attached to the immediate motivation behind the reproduction or distribution itself, rather than to the ultimate profit-making motivation of the enterprise in which the library is located.

The library can charge for the cost of making the copy without having "commercial advantage" as a purpose, but, once the library makes any significant profit on a copy or uses copying as a way of defraying other expenses, there is an immediate profit motive attached to the making or distribution of the copy.

**Notice of copyright must appear on the copy.** All copies distributed or reproduced by libraries or archives must include the notice of copyright to qualify under Section 108. If copies or phonorecords fail to include the appropriate notice, the library might cause an unknowing party to reasonably assume the work is in the public domain because of the lack of notice.

**No more than one copy may be made.** Libraries cannot make multiple copies, except under special conditions. The first exception is outside Section 108. In certain circumstances and for certain purposes, it may be possible to make multiple copies under the fair-use doctrine. Under Section 108, the general rule is "no more than one copy or phonorecord." However, a library may copy the same material more than once if the reproductions are "isolated and unrelated" and are "single" copies made on "separate occasions." Thus, if the library copies an article from a periodical in January for one user, the copying of the same article for a second user in

March would not destroy the library exemption—unless the library was aware that such reproduction was related or done in concert. A specific exemption permitting multiple copies *in some circumstances* for interlibrary arrangements is also explained in Section 108.

**Making the copy cannot violate an agreement.** The limitation on a copyright owner's exclusive rights, specified in Section 108, does not prevent the copyright owner from entering into a contract or agreement with the library in which the library agrees not to make reproductions or distribute copies as a condition of obtaining a copy of the work from the author. Undoubtedly, such contracts are more common in connection with unpublished works, but the library exemption from copyright infringement does not permit the library to reproduce copies in violation of an agreement to the contrary. If a library has entered into such an agreement, it would seem prudent, although not required by statute, that a notice to that effect be placed directly on the work that is the subject of the agreement.

# Copies Made for the Library's Own Use (or Use by Another Library)

The statute distinguishes between copies made for a library's own use and those made for the use of a patron of the library. The reproductions permitted for the library's own use, or for use by another library, are more extensive and can be divided into two classes:

1. *Unpublished Works*—A copy of the entire work can be made *if* the library currently has a copy in its collection *and* the reproduction is made for the purpose of preservation and security of the material, *or* for the purpose of deposit for research use in another library.

2. *Published Works*—A copy of the entire work can be made, but only for the purpose of replacement of a damaged, deteriorated, lost, or stolen copy, and *only if* a reasonable effort has been made by the library to find and acquire an unused replacement at a fair price.

Therefore, unpublished works can be copied by libraries for preservation, while published works can be copied by libraries for replacement, when they are not otherwise available at a fair price. These limitations on a copyright owner's exclusive rights are generally not going to be burdensome, and attempts to widen these limitations are not likely to be well received, particularly if an improper purpose or motive is discovered relating to the library reproduction or distribution.

## Copies Made by the Library for Library Users

***Types of work that may be reproduced.*** The right of libraries to reproduce copies for their users is initially limited to essentially textual works. A library cannot copy musical, pictorial, graphic, or sculptural works, or motion pictures for its users and qualify for an exemption under Section 108. It can make copies of such works for its own use, but not for use by library patrons. If an essentially written or textual work includes illustration, diagrams, and "similar adjuncts," reproduction *will* be permitted. Thus, an attempt has been made to draw a line between works in which the nontext portions are incidental and those in which the nontext material constitutes the work. The former can be copied; the latter cannot. Again, it should be noted that copying of such nontext works *might* be permissible as fair use, but not under the library exemption.

In addition to the limitation that copies for library users must be essentially textual in nature, the copies also must be owned by the library users for the purpose of private study, scholarship, or research. The library cannot keep or require return of the copies made. If the library is aware that the user is not going to use the copy for study, scholarship, or research, it should not make the copy.

***Warning to library users.*** The library must place a notice warning the user of possible copyright infringement *both* on the order form ("Order Warning of Copyright") and conspicuously at the place of ordering ("Display Warning of Copyright"). The regula-

tions adopted by the Copyright Office (Regulations Section 201.14) require the following notice:

> The copyright law of the United States (Title 17, United States Code) governs the making of photocopies or other reproductions of copyrighted material.
>
> Under certain conditions specified in the law, libraries and archives are authorized to furnish a photocopy or other reproduction. One of these specified conditions is that the photocopy or reproduction is not to be "used for any purpose other than private study, scholarship, or research." If a user makes a request for, or later uses, a photocopy or reproduction for purposes in excess of "fair use," that user may be liable for copyright infringement.
>
> This institution reserves the right to refuse to accept a copying order if, in its judgment, fulfillment of the order would involve violation of copyright law.

**Conditions that permit copying.** If the above conditions for reproduction of copies for library users are met, libraries can make copies in the following two situations: first, when, "no more than one article or other contribution to a copyrighted collection or periodical issue, or . . . a small part of any other copyrighted work" is reproduced; *or*, second, when the entire work or a substantial portion is reproduced, if reasonable investigation by the library enables determination that the work cannot be obtained at a fair price.

The first situation is essentially coextensive with the doctrine of fair use. Thus, for scholarly purposes, copying one article from a periodical usually would be permitted under Section 107 dealing with fair use. The problem, of course, under fair use is determining what is "small." The second situation enables complete works to be copied without *library* copyright infringement, if *investigation* by the library indicates copies cannot be obtained at a fair price. Obviously, some experience will be required to draw the line between "fair" and "unfair" prices.

Libraries can make a copy for their users of articles, portions of works, and complete works, when they are not available at a fair price, *if* the work is essentially textual, the copy will be owned by the library patron, warning notices are given, and the copy is to be used for scholarly purposes. Again, the limitation on the copyright owner's exclusive rights to copies made by libraries for their users is relatively modest.

**Audiovisual news programs.** The interest of disseminating news was felt to be strong enough to justify greater latitude in connection with audiovisual news programs. A library may reproduce and distrubute *by lending* a limited number of copies of audiovisual news programs or excerpts. For example, multiple copies can be made by off-the-air taping and distributed, as long as the distribution is by lending. The library, not the library user, must be the ultimate owner of the copies, and the material reproduced must be an audiovisual news program.

## Unsupervised Library Photocopy Machines

**Library responsibility.** As stated at the beginning of this chapter, Section 108 is for the benefit of libraries, not library users. One of the provisions of Section 108 most likely to be misunderstood is that *libraries* will be exempt from copyright infringement as a result of reproductions made by library patrons at an unsupervised photocopy machine on the library premises, if the proper warning notices are present. Library *users* will *not* be exempt. From the copyright owner's viewpoint, this limitation creates a loophole in his or her exclusive rights. From the library's point of view, this immunity greatly reduces the incentive for library personnel to do any copying for library users. Investigations as to "fair" price, consideration of how much is a "small" part of a work, and queries as to whether the user's purpose is scholarly can all be eliminated by directing the patron to the unsupervised copy machine.

The copyright owner, theoretically, could sue infringers who go beyond fair use at the unsupervised library photocopy machine, but as a practical matter, policing is impossible. Conversely, however, it is often less economical to make an infringing copy at the library photocopy machine than to purchase the same material at a bookstore. Until and unless photocopy machines are licensed in a manner similar to jukeboxes, the policy is that society has a legitimate interest in having unsupervised photocopying available at libraries for scholarly endeavors, and, accordingly, that libraries should not be exposed to copyright infringement in providing such facilities. The potential benefit was thought to outweigh the potential abuse, particularly when the copyright owner retains the theoretical ability to stop abuse.

**Liability for infringement.** What happens to the library or library employee who misinterprets the guidelines with regard to questions such as "small part" or purposes of "private study, scholarship, or research"? Section 504 of the Copyright Act specifically prohibits awarding damages when an employee or representative of a library, archive, or nonprofit educational institution infringes a copyright, if the party "had reasonable grounds for believing that his or her use of the copyrighted work was a fair use under Section 107."

While Section 504 solves the problem for libraries and librarians—*but not library users*—situations relating to fair use under Section 107, the protection from liability elaborated in Section 504 is not specifically applicable to Section 108. There is some danger, therefore, that a misinterpretation by a library employee of what constitutes a "fair" price under Section 108 could give rise to liability on the part of the library for damages. Section 504, however, does authorize a court to reduce damages to not less than $100 if the infringer was innocent—that is, the infringer had no reason to believe that the act of copying would be an infringement.

Generally, neither the library nor librarians will be significantly liable for copyright infringement if they attempt, in good faith, to follow the provisions of sections 107 and 108.

# 7 copyright exemptions for nonprofit, governmental, and religious uses

There are specific exceptions to a copyright owner's exclusive rights to the control and use of his or her work. The exceptions made under the fair-use doctrine are covered in Chapter 4 of this book. In addition, liberal allowances are made when the work is used for nonprofit purposes, especially if they benefit educational, religious, governmental or charitable institutions, or the handicapped. These limitations on a copyright owner's rights are primarily confined to the areas of public performance and public display of a work. There are a few exceptions that affect the exclusive rights to reproduce, distribute copies, or to make derivative works.

The copyright owner's exclusive performance-and-display rights extend only to *public* performances and displays. Thus, no exemption is required for the private performance or display of a work. A performance or display is public if it is at a place open to the public *or* any place where a substantial number of persons other than family and/or social acquaintances are gathered. It is also public if the performance or display is transmitted by radio, television, or other methods to public places—even though the public may be in separate locations (watching separate television sets) or receives the transmission at separate times.

The playing of a phonorecord on which a musical composition is recorded *is* a performance. If that performance is public, the copyright in the musical composition has been infringed unless there is an exemption or limitation permitting the performance. Under the old law, the performance had to be in public *and* "for profit." The for-profit requirement has been removed from the basic, exclusive right to control public performances, but many of the exemptions require nonprofit performances.

## Limitations in Favor of Nonprofit Educational Institutions

Specific limitations on the exclusive rights comprising copyright benefit nonprofit educational institutions. The primary exemption is directed toward performance or display of *any type of work* by instructors or pupils in the course of face-to-face *teaching* activities. This exemption does not extend to recreational or nonteaching activities, nor is it currently available to profit-making educational organizations. Additionally, the performance or display must be in a face-to-face situation. Video teaching is covered by another specific exception discussed below. Only teachers and pupils may perform or display.

There are additional exemptions for educational transmissions by radio, television, or the like. The performance of *nondramatic* literary or musical works or the display of any type of work by transmission is exempt if (1) it is part of the systematic instructional activities of a nonprofit educational institution; *and* (2) the performance or display is directly related and of material assistance to a teaching content; *and* (3) the transmission is for reception in classrooms or by the disabled or governmental employees.

Thus, a nonprofit educational institution can broadcast or transmit *nondramatic* works, but dramatic works can only be performed in face-to-face situations. Moreover, one-time, nonsystematic teaching activities by educational institutions or broadcasts to non-classroom locations will not be exempt.

It also is possible for educational institutions to give fund-raising performances of nondramatic literary or musical works. The performers, promoters, and organizers must not receive a fee, and the performance cannot be for commercial gain. Payment of a teacher/performer of his or her ordinary salary will not destroy the exemption. The proceeds after costs must be used for educational purposes. As in other fund-raising situations, however, the copyright owner can prohibit the performance by serving a notice at least seven days before the performance is to take place. Plays are dramatic works and do not fall into this category; they require licenses.

## Limitations in Favor of Governmental Bodies

The performance of nondramatic literary or musical works or the display of any type of work by transmission through a governmental body as part of systematic instructional activities will be exempt from copyright infringement—if it is material to the teaching content and is transmitted to classrooms, disabled persons, or government employees as part of their official duties. Transmissions related to recreational activities and dramatic works are not exempt. Governmental bodies are not specifically exempt for face-to-face teaching situations, although most are clearly nonprofit. It seems likely that a governmental body could be considered a nonprofit educational institution in face-to-face situations for the performance of nondramatic works. However, until this is resolved, *transmission* of the performance of the nondramatic work is safer.

Secondary transmissions of primary broadcasts by a governmental body without commercial gain or the charge of a fee, other than to defray costs, are also exempt from copyright infringement.

In addition, governmental bodies are exempt from copyright infringement in the performance of nondramatic musical works at an annual agricultural or horticultural fair or exhibition. This exemption does not include nondramatic literary work nor fairs or exhibitions outside the agricultural or horticultural area. The exemption extends to the governmental body for music performed by concessionaires, but not to the concessionaires themselves.

## Limitations in Favor of Religious Organizations

The primary exception to copyright infringement favoring religious organizations is the ability to perform nondramatic literary or musical works during religious services *in a place of worship*. Additionally, dramatic *musical* works can be performed during religious services in a place of worship if the dramatic musical composition is religious in nature. Finally, any type of copyrighted work can be displayed during the course of a religious service in the place of worship.

This exemption does not extend to performances or displays outside of religious services or at locations other than the place of worship. Moreover, unless a dramatic work is religious, the exemption does not extend to performance of the dramatic work.

Thus, religious fund raisers, benefits, and radio and television broadcasts that do not take place during services or in the place of worship are not covered by the general limitation favoring religious organizations.

It is possible, however, to obtain an exemption from copyright infringement for religious fund-raising programs. The performance of nondramatic literary or musical works other than by transmission (television, for instance) will be exempt under certain circumstances. The purpose of the performance cannot be. direct or indirect *commercial* advantage, and the performers, promoters, and organizers cannot receive a fee or compensation. Additionally, there must be no admission charge, or the proceeds after costs must be used exclusively for "education, religious, or charitable purposes and not for private financial gain."

However, the copyright owner can prevent performances, even if they otherwise qualify, by serving a written notice on the organizers at least seven days before the performance.

Religious organizations, therefore, have an exemption in connection with the performance of certain works and the display of works during services. They also may be eligible to perform nondramatic works during fund raisers, but they will be required to negotiate licenses with the copyright owners if these limited exemptions from copyright infringement do not cover their activities.

## Limitations in Favor of Others

Public performances arranged by charitable institutions, either as fund raisers or simply as a public service, can be exempt. The performance must be of nondramatic literary or musical works, and, as in educational and religious performances, there can be no fees paid to the performers or promoters. Additionally, there must be no admission charge, or if there is a charge, the proceeds must be used for charitable purposes. Again, copyright owners can prohibit such performances by serving written notice on the organizers at least seven days before the performance.

As with governmental exemptions, nonprofit agricultural or horticultural organizations are exempt from copyright infringement for the performance of nondramatic musical works at annual fairs or exhibitions.

Music stores and the like are exempt from infringement for public performances of nondramatic musical works on their premises for the promotion of retail sales of phonorecords. There must be no admission charge, and the performance cannot be transmitted beyond the store.

The performance by transmission of a nondramatic literary work or a published, ten-year-old dramatic literary work is exempt, if it is directed *primarily* to the blind or deaf, is made without any purpose of direct or indirect commercial advantage, *and* is made through the facilities of a governmental body or noncommercial, educational broadcast station, radio subcarrier, or cable system.

## Limitations on the Exclusive Right to Reproduce

Generally, an organization that is *licensed* to perform or display a work by transmitting, for example, by radio or television, will be entitled to make at least one copy or reproduction of the work. This ability to make a copy, however, does not extend to motion pictures or other audiovisual works, nor does it extend to all of the exempt situations just described. Once a *license* to transmit is granted, it will automatically include permission to make *one* copy if the copy is retained by the transmitting organization, used solely for transmission in the local area or for archival purposes, *and*—unless preserved exclusively for archival purposes—if it is destroyed within six months of the first transmission.

If the transmission is not the result of a license, but an exemption, copies can also be made if a governmental or nonprofit organization is involved; no more than thirty copies are made; and all but one copy is destroyed within seven years. Additionally, governmental and nonprofit institutions can make copies of nondramatic musical works of a religious nature for certain purposes, and can make copies of nondramatic literary works for the blind and deaf under certain conditions.

None of the copies made under these exemptions shall be entitled to copyright protection as derivative works, unless the copyright owner of the preexisting work agrees to such protection.

## Cable Television and Noncommercial Broadcasting

The Copyright Act contains exemptions or limitations on the exclusive rights comprising copyright that favor cable television and noncommercial broadcasting. These exceptions are extremely complex, but in general, they tend to be applicable only to published works and either exempt or create compulsory licenses for performances and displays. Such compulsory licenses may be either royalty free or based upon a royalty established by the Copyright Royalty Tribunal. Collection of such compulsory-license royalties requires the copyright owner to make a claim with the Copyright Royalty Tribunal—discussed in Chapter 5 under "Royalties, Compulsory Licensing, and the Copyright Royalty Tribunal."

# APPENDIX I
## major changes in the new copyright law

The Copyright Act of 1976 can probably be more accurately described as an entirely new body of law rather than as an amendment or revision of the Copyright Act of 1909. Summarizing the changes, therefore, is difficult and further complicated by the fact that in many instances the "old" copyright law is effective.

Perhaps the most basic change in the new law is the strengthening of the rights of authors and the deemphasis of the rights of publishers. This philosophical shifting of rights appears in many provisions of the new law.

With the caution that summary statements can be misleading and should not be regarded as a substitute for the more detailed treatment of subjects elsewhere in this book, the following summarizes fifteen major changes in the new law:

1.  SINGLE SYSTEM OF COPYRIGHT LAW
    The old law was based upon a dual system of copyright protection. Federal statutory law (essentially for published works) and state common-law copyright (for unpublished works). The new Copyright Act substitutes a single, federal statutory law for both published and unpublished works.
2.  AUTOMATIC PROTECTION UPON CREATION
    The new Copyright Act provides that a work is automatically protected upon "creation," that is, fixation of the work in a tangible medium. You do not have to publish or register a work to be entitled to copyright protection. Copyright registration, however, provides important rights and remedies.

3.  DIVISIBLE COPYRIGHT

    Any one of the group of rights comprising the copyright in a work can be divided from and dealt with independently of the remaining rights.

4.  AUTHORS RETAIN ALL RIGHTS NOT EXPRESSLY TRANSFERRED

    The presumption under the new law is that an author retains all of the rights in a work except those that are expressly transferred.

5.  TRANSFERS MUST BE WRITTEN

    Other than nonexclusive licenses, all transfers of a copyright must be written to be enforceable. Oral exclusive licenses and assignments of a copyright are not valid.

6.  DURATION OF COPYRIGHT

    The length or duration of copyright has been extended substantially. The basic term is now the life of the author plus fifty years. For certain other works, most important, works "for hire," the term is the shorter of seventy-five years from publication or one hundred years from creation. The term of existing copyrights has also been extended.

7.  COPYRIGHT RENEWAL

    The renewal requirement of the old law has been largely, but not completely, eliminated. Those copyrights that must be renewed can be renewed for a longer term than in the past.

8.  TRANSFERS CAN BE TERMINATED

    Exclusive and nonexclusive licenses and assignments can be terminated by an author or certain heirs at the author's election, even though the license agreement or assignment expressly purports to prohibit termination by the author. For works licensed or assigned after 1977, the right of the author to terminate becomes effective between thirty-five and forty years after grant of the license or assignment.

9.  WORKS MADE FOR HIRE REQUIRE A WRITTEN INSTRUMENT

    Unless an author is working within the scope of his or her employment, a written document signed by the author is required before a work will be deemed to have been a "work made for hire" and thereby owned by the employer. Works that are orally ordered or commissioned from nonemployee authors are owned by the author of the work, not the person or business ordering them.

10. ERRORS IN THE COPYRIGHT NOTICE

Errors that are made in the copyright notice required upon publication of a work can be corrected for a period of up to five years from first publication of the work. Even complete omission of the notice can now be corrected. Previously, publication without the proper notice would cause the work to fall into the public domain.

11. PANTOMIMES, CHOREOGRAPHY, AND COMPUTER PROGRAMS

Pantomimes and choreography reduced to a tangible form, such as by notation, are now expressly subject to the new Copyright Act. Computer programs and data bases are also protectable.

12. "FAIR USE" OF COPYRIGHTED WORKS IS DEFINED

The law has provided statutory guidelines as to what constitutes noninfringing fair use of a copyrighted work. The new statutory law attempts to state, rather than change, the old case law.

13. COMPULSORY COPYRIGHT LICENSES ARE ENLARGED

The old law provided for compulsory licensing for phonorecords. These compulsory licenses are continued at a new, higher, royalty rate. Compulsory licensing of copyrighted works for use in jukeboxes, secondary transmissions (cable systems), and noncommercial broadcasts has been added by the new law.

14. COPYRIGHT ROYALTY TRIBUNAL

A new administrative court was created primarily to administer the distribution of royalties under the compulsory licensing provisions.

15. MANUFACTURE IN THE UNITED STATES

The requirement for manufacture of nondramatic English-language literary works in the United States has been liberalized and will be completely eliminated by July 1, 1982.

There are many other important changes in the law, including changes relating to library photocopying, cable television, and educational, religious, and nonprofit uses of copyrighted works. Moreover, vast administrative changes have been implemented by the Copyright Office including a dramatic reduction in the number of classes of works for registration, the creation of entirely new copyright forms, increases in the Copyright Office fees, and changes in the deposit requirements.

While numerous changes have resulted from the Copyright Act of 1976, many of these changes make it more feasible for the nonattorney author to register a claim to copyright and to place a proper notice on the work.

# APPENDIX II
## forms of protection other than copyright

Copyright is not the only form of legal protection for intellectual property. In addition to the copyright law, intellectual creations may be protectable under patent, trade-secret, and unfair-competition laws, or a combination of these laws. It is beyond the scope of this book to thoroughly examine the similarities and differences among each of these bodies of law. You should realize, however, that these laws are founded upon entirely different bases, and while they may appear to overlap to some extent, they are significantly different in the scope and nature of the rights protected.

### Patents

You cannot assume that registering a claim to copyright on your innovation or invention will preserve your patent rights until you get around to applying for a patent. Registering a claim to copyright on a patentable invention is probably worse than a meaningless act. Your claim to copyright on the *description* will be registered by the Copyright Office, giving you a feeling of security, but the copyright registration will not prevent someone from *using the invention*. Moreover, by the time you realize that the copyright protection for the description of your invention only prevents others from *copying the description*, you may discover that it is too late to obtain valid patent rights. If you have what you think may be a patentable invention, you should see a patent attorney.

Generally, technological, scientific, and utilitarian works can be protected by patents, while creations of the "arts," in the broad sense, are subject to copyright protection. There are three types of patents: utility patents, design patents, and plant patents. Any person who invents or discovers a new and *useful* process, machine, manufacture, or composition of matter, or any new and useful improvement of these, may obtain a *utility* patent. Inventive, new, ornamental designs for manufactured articles may be protected by *design* patents. Design-patent protection and copyright protection are both often available for three-dimensional works of artistic craftsmanship. Accordingly, some further examination of this area of the law can be found in the subsection of Chapter 5 entitled "Design Patents and Copyrights." *Plant* patents are granted for new and distinct varieties of plants that are discovered and asexually reproduced, that is, mutants or hybrids that can be reproduced only by grafting or taking a slip from the original mutant plant.

## Trade Secrets

Trade secrets, confidential information and know-how, are usually more closely related to patents than copyrights. They lend themselves more to the protection of technological and utilitarian creations than artistic, literary, or musical creations. Unlike patents, trade secrets do not require inventiveness; they are founded upon the maintenance of secrecy or confidentiality of information. Usually, the manner in which the information is expressed is not the essence of the secret. Computer-program developers, however, often try to protect their programs under either or both the copyright and trade-secret laws, since the manner of expressing the program for a generally known concept can still constitute a valuable trade secret. One of the unresolved questions created by the Copyright Act of 1976 is whether trade-secret protection is still available to works that are copyrightable in nature.

## Unfair Competition

The law of unfair competition includes the trademark law. A trademark is a word, name, symbol, device, or any combination of the four, used to identify the source or origin of products. The trademark must not merely describe or identify the product; it must indicate a single source of the product. Service marks similarly indicate the origin of services. A trademark owner can prevent competitors from using a similar or identical trademark if the mark used by the competitor would be likely to cause confusion among consumers. Thus, if consumers are likely to think that the competitor's product comes from the trademark owner, the competitor has competed with the trademark owner unfairly. Both copyright and trademark protection can be available in connection with advertising materials, such as product labels and distinctive product containers.

## Procedural Differences

In addition to the differences between the copyright, patent, trade-secret, and unfair-competition laws themselves, there are considerable differences between the respective procedures for preserving these rights. Copyright protection automatically comes into existence upon creation of the work, and registration of a claim to copyright with the United States Copyright Office is relatively easy and inexpensive. Patent protection is not automatic, and it requires the filing of a patent application with the United States Patent and Trademark Office before issuance of a patent. The procedure is complex and costly, as compared to copyright registration, and it usually should be done by a patent attorney.

Trade-secret protection requires a constant effort to maintain the secrecy of the subject matter. There is no formal registration, application, or certification procedure. Trademarks can be enforced without registration, but registration gives some substantial advantages, just as it does with copyrights. A trademark can be registered on a national level with the United States Patent and Trademark Office or on a local level with state trademark offices. The procedure is somewhat more costly and complex than copyright registration, but it is simpler than obtaining a patent.

Differences also exist with regard to the timing of the steps necessary for protection. While it is possible (although usually not advisable) to delay registration of a claim to copyright for many years without adverse effects, a delay in filing a patent application can be disastrous. Under the United States laws, you must file your patent application within one year of the first public use, printed publication, or offer for sale of the invention. If you do not, your patent rights will be irretrievably lost. Moreover, in most foreign countries you cannot wait one year; you must have filed the patent application before any public use, publication, or offer for sale of the invention *anywhere in the world*.

Accordingly, you cannot assume that registering a claim to copyright will protect all of these various rights. It will not. It will perfect those exclusive rights that comprise your copyright, but if you believe your intellectual creation may be protectable under other laws, you should immediately pursue such protection.

# APPENDIX III
## resource
# information

## The Copyright Office

The mailing address of the Copyright Office is: United States Copyright Office, Library of Congress, Washington, D.C. 20559.

***The Copyright Information and Publications Section.*** If you have a specific question or need advice on completing your application for copyright registration, the Copyright Office Information and Publications Section provides this service free of charge. If your question is of a general nature, send a letter and you will probably receive a printed circular relating to the particular subject. If your problem is unique, you may have to telephone in order to obtain the information you need. The Copyright Office is not permitted to give legal opinions or advice, but it can give you considerable information concerning your particular area of interest. Write to the Information and Publications Section at the address above, or call (202) 287-8700.

***Copyright Office circulars and other printed information.*** The Copyright Office publishes a number of circulars each year relating to various aspects of copyright law and procedure. You can obtain a free list of currently available publications by writing to the Copyright Office at the address above.

# Copyright Search

If you want to make a search of the official records of the Copyright Office, you may do so Monday through Friday, except holidays, between 8 A.M. and 4 P.M. There is no charge. The location is: Copyright Office, James Madison Building, First and Independence S.E., Washington, D.C.

Please note this is not the mailing address for the Copyright Office, but the actual location. There are no branch offices in other locations at which you can conduct a search. However, you can obtain information based on the official records by reference to the *Catalog of Copyright Entries*, or you can have the Copyright Office make a search for you. Your attorney can also arrange for searching by means of private searching services in Washington, D.C.

**Catalog of Copyright Entries.** These books are published by the Copyright Office on a regular basis. They list all registrations and renewals for specific time periods and give the essential facts. They do not cover assignments or transfers. These books are available in many libraries throughout the country.

**Search by the Copyright Office.** If you want the Copyright Office to make a search for you, first you should write for an estimate of the total cost. Send as much information as possible on which the Office can base its estimate. Include, if possible, all known titles of the work; the name of author or pseudonym used; the name of copyright owner; the approximate date of publication or registration; the type of work, such as book or sound recording; the registration number; and, if the work was a contribution to a collective work, the name and date of the collection or periodical in which it appeared. Also state whether your search request is in reference to a registration, a renewal, an assignment, or another type of document. The Copyright Office will send you an estimated fee based upon the estimated search time and a search rate of $10 per hour. You can then instruct the Copyright Office to proceed with the search, should you so decide.

## Patents and Trademark Office

The United States Patent and Trademark Office and the United States Copyright Office are entirely separate government agencies. The Copyright Office cannot furnish you with information concerning patents and trademarks. However, you can obtain free brochures on these subjects by writing to the Commissioner of Patents, Washington, D.C. 20231. The general-information number for the Patent and Trademark Office is (703) 557-3080.

# Index